THE GOSPELS
a first commentary

F.G. HEROD

JOHN KNOX PRESS
ATLANTA

The cover photograph, "Christ in Majesty"
from the Cotton M.S. Vespasian
is by courtesy of the Trustees of the British Museum

First published in Great Britain by Methuen Educational Ltd 1976
Published in U.S.A. by John Knox Press 1977

Library of Congress Cataloging in Publication Data
Herod, Frederic George.
 The Gospels.
 Bibliography: p.
 Includes indexes.
 1. Bible. N.T. Gospels—Criticism, interpretation,
etc. I. Title.
BS2555.2.H43 1977   266'.07   77-79590
ISBN 0-8042-0255-9

Printed in the U.S.A.
John Knox Press
Atlanta, Georgia

Contents

Foreword

This commentary is intended to interest students who are
studying the gospels in detail for the first time. It should be used
side by side with the Bible text.

Matters of textual criticism and general authenticity, apart
from a simple outline of the Synoptic Problem, are not introduced,
because the author has primarily in mind the needs of students
taking a variety of secondary examinations in this subject.

All three Synoptic Gospels are covered and the reader who is
studying selected passages should have no difficulty in finding
them in the commentary. With regard to the Fourth Gospel
comment has been restricted to general details and to passages
linked with the Synoptics together with some other outstanding
events recorded in St. John (see page 73).

The chronological order is based mainly on St. Mark, and the
placing of passages peculiar to the other two gospels as, for
instance, the Sermon on the Mount, has no special significance.

The author's own students have used these notes for many
years and he hopes that they will continue to be a help in passing
examinations and will also foster a lively interest in the gospel
and its message for mankind.

One Solitary Life

Here is a man who was born in an obscure village, the child of a peasant woman. He grew up in another obscure village. He worked in a carpenter's shop until he was thirty, and then for three years he was an itinerant preacher. He never wrote a book. He never held an office. He never owned a home. He never had a family. He never went to college. He never put his foot inside a big city. He never travelled two hundred miles [322 km] from the place where he was born. He never did any of the things that usually accompany greatness.

While still a young man, the tide of popular opinion turned against him. His friends ran away. One of them denied him. He was turned over to his enemies. He went through the mockery of a trial. He was nailed to a cross between two thieves. While he was dying his executioners gambled for the only piece of property he had on earth and that was his coat. When he was dead he was taken down and laid in a borrowed grave through the pity of a friend. . .

Yet I am far within the mark when I say that all the armies that have ever marched and all the navies that ever were built, and all the parliaments that ever sat, and all the kings that ever reigned, put together have not affected the life of man upon this earth as powerfully as has that **one solitary life.**

James A. Francis

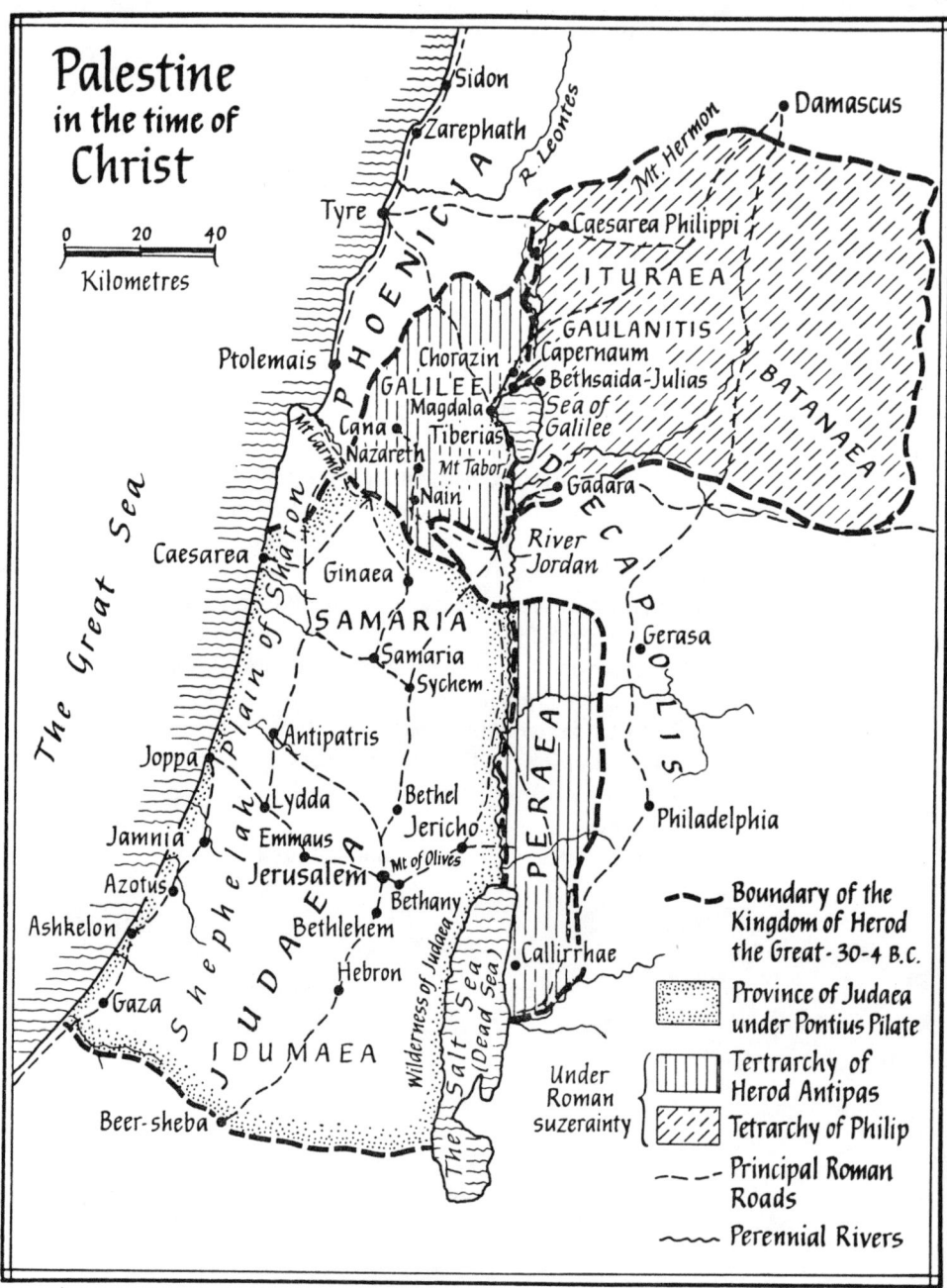

Palestine in the time of Christ

0 20 40
Kilometres

Sidon
Zarephath
R. Leontes
Damascus
Tyre
Caesarea Philippi
PHOENICIA
ITURAEA
Mt Hermon
GAULANITIS
Chorazin
Capernaum
GALILEE
Bethsaida-Julias
Magdala
BATANAEA
Cana
Sea of Galilee
Tiberias
Ptolemais
Nazareth
Mt Carmel
Mt Tabor
Nain
Gadara
DECAPOLIS
Caesarea
River Jordan
Ginaea
SAMARIA
Plain of Sharon
Gerasa
Samaria
Sychem
Antipatris
Joppa
Lydda
Bethel
Jericho
PERAEA
Philadelphia
Emmaus
Jamnia
Shephelah
Mt of Olives
Azotus
Jerusalem
Bethany
Ashkelon
Bethlehem
JUDAEA
Callirrhoe
Hebron
The Great Sea
Gaza
Wilderness of Judaea
The Salt Sea (Dead Sea)
IDUMAEA
Beer-sheba

– – – Boundary of the Kingdom of Herod the Great - 30-4 B.C.

Province of Judaea under Pontius Pilate

Under Roman suzerainty { Tetrarchy of Herod Antipas / Tetrarchy of Philip

– – – Principal Roman Roads

～～ Perennial Rivers

Palestine

If you look at the map opposite this page, you will see that at the time of Christ Palestine consisted of a number of separate provinces. The Gospel story is concerned almost entirely with only three of them, Galilee, Samaria and Judaea. For government purposes Samaria and Judaea went under the general title of Judaea. In these three provinces Jesus lived and worked and only on rare occasions did he go outside them.

Galilee

Galilee in the north was the most prosperous. Vines, olives, cereals and fruit grew there in abundance. One traveller recently reported that he walked down a lane ankle d⌒ep in fig juice! The countryside, rich in wild flowers, was grazed by thousands of sheep tended lovingly by shepherds twenty-four hours of the day. The Sea of Galilee (Lake of Genneseret or Sea of Tiberias) was a great fishing ground on which as many as four thousand fishing vessels could be seen at one time. Much of this fish was salted and despatched to other parts of the Roman Empire. On the edge of the sea stood Capernaum, Christ's teaching centre, an important city with a customs house and a Roman barracks.

The Galileans were a tough, independent people who resented being governed from Jerusalem, the capital. The province was a breeding ground for rebellion against the Romans.

Judaea

Judaea in the south was mountainous and poorer than Galilee, though politically more important as it included the capital, Jerusalem. This very holy city contained a beautiful temple, the High Priest's palace, a Roman fort and many colleges for the training of rabbis. The people of Jerusalem felt themselves superior to anyone who came, for instance, from a Galilean town or village such as Nazareth. Especially was this so, because the haughty Judaeans accused the Galileans of inter-marriage with non-Jews and despised them for their crude manners and speech (cf., the servant girl and Peter, Matt. 26, 69-73).

Samaria

Samaria, situated between Galilee and Judaea, was out of bounds for the strict Jew. Its inhabitants were of mixed stock, only partly Jewish, and therefore despised by the Sons of Abraham, especially

1

the Judaeans. The Samaritans accepted the first five books of the Old Testament - the 'Books of Moses' - as Law, but their worship though similar to the Jews' had alien elements also. They scorned any association with the Jews (cf., their treatment of Jesus, Luke 9, 51-56) and delighted in isolated acts of hostility, such as seizing a lonely Jewish traveller and selling him into slavery.

The Romans

The Romans had occupied Palestine for sixty years before Christ was born. They had been invited into the country to restore order by a strict Jewish sect known as the Pharisees, who soon afterwards regretted their action. The Romans allowed the Jews to keep their own religious laws and customs provided they also kept the peace and paid their taxes, which were collected by publicans (tax-collectors) who were generally hated for their dishonesty. The official language was Greek; the language of the common people, Aramaic.

The Romans were disliked because they were Gentiles (non-Jews) and therefore 'unclean'; they were arrogant - a Roman soldier, for example, could force a Jew to carry his pack for one Roman mile (1.48 km); they were cruel, especially in their punishment of revolutionaries; and they introduced pagan temples and customs into the country.

Herod the Great

Herod the Great was ruler of Palestine when Jesus was born. He maintained very friendly relationships with the Emperors who reigned during his lifetime. They, in fact, extended his territory because he was clearly a most competent ruler, and this despite the almost unbearable plotting and intrigue he had to face amongst his own family and friends.

He was a very jealous husband. When he had to leave home, he had his wife, Mariamne, a very beautiful girl, made virtually a prisoner and gave orders that if he did not return, she should be put to death immediately. She did not care much for this treatment! She and her mother, Alexandra, who hated her son-in-law, seemed always to be at the centre of some intrigue, so that finally, when he thought he had discovered evidence of Mariamne's adultery, he had them both put to death. Two of his sons also plotted against him and they suffered a similar fate. His worst enemies were those of his own household.

As a ruler he was clever, cunning (cf., his treatment of the wise men, Matthew 2), resourceful and cruel (cf., his massacre of the Bethlehem children, Matthew 2).

He had a great love of architecture. He built the third and last temple in Jerusalem to please the Jews and then infuriated them by building pagan temples elsewhere. He was, in any case, despised by them because he was only half-Jewish by blood.

He died on April 1, 4B.C. from cancer of the intestines.

After his death his territory was divided among his three sons, Antipas, Philip and Archelaus. The last of these was deposed by the Emperor for cruelty and inefficiency. As a consequence, during Christ's ministry Pontius Pilate, a Roman procurator, also much hated by the Jews for his cruelty, ruled Judaea while Herod Antipas continued to rule Galilee.

The Jewish state
  Though the Romans ruled Palestine as part of the Empire and took a great deal of wealth out of the country they found it advisable to allow the Jews to govern themselves as far as possible in religious and social matters.

To the Jews, God was head of the state and their High Priest his representative on earth. You can imagine their angry resentment when Rome deposed their High Priest, Annas, and appointed his son-in-law, Caiaphas, in his place. Secretly, they would never acknowledge this and that is why, according to two gospels, Jesus after his arrest was brought before Annas before he was taken to Caiaphas. But Caiaphas in Christ's day was responsible directly to the Roman authorities for the conduct of his people.

To a proud people like the Jews, this servitude to the Romans was intolerable. They believed that God would soon send them a deliverer (Hebrew: Messiah) who would set them free. For most people, therefore, the coming of the Messiah would be a signal for armed rebellion. Messiah would be a second David, a warrior and a liberator.

As we realise, Jesus had a quite different view of messiahship. That is why during his period of popularity in Galilee, he never referred to himself as Messiah (except indirectly in Nazareth) for fear of provoking revolution. He called himself 'Son of Man' and identified himself with the 'Suffering Servant' of Isaiah 53, 2-9.

The Jewish place of worship was the synagogue to be found in every village and town (note - there was only *one* Temple - in Jerusalem). Every male Jew was expected to attend synagogue on the Sabbath which began at sundown on Friday and ended twenty-four hours later. Women were welcome to attend the services but they sat separately from the men. The chief officials of each synagogue formed a local council which was responsible to see

3

that the Law of Moses was observed at all times by the congregation.

Whilst the men were responsible for the maintenance of the synagogue - twelve had to be present before a service could be held - the women were responsible for the religious life of the family at home. They prepared each week for the Sabbath, and also for the many festivals throughout the year. The chief of these was the Passover, celebrated in the springtime. It commemorated the Israelite escape from slavery in Egypt (c. 1200B.C.) as described in the Book of Exodus (Ex. 12, 12-36).

The Law which governed the social and religious life of the Jews was contained in the first five books of the Old Testament, and called the Torah. This was the Law of Moses which could not be challenged and was therefore unalterable.

The Scribes

The Scribes (lawyers) interpreted the Law and acted as Judges and lawyers in the Jewish courts, the chief of which was the Sanhedrin in Jerusalem, before which Christ was tried.

The Scribes were also teachers of the Law and many of them had groups of followers - disciples. We know the names of some of the most distinguished in New Testament times: Hillel, Shammai, Gamaliel. From the Law of Moses they had developed the 'Traditions of the Elders' or the 'Oral Law'. This was their collective interpretation of the Law of Moses (for example, the meaning of work on the Sabbath). Unfortunately, this Oral Law in Christ's day consisted of over six hundred rules for personal guidance. In addition, there were different interpretations according to which famous teacher you selected, So, in fact, the Law had developed quite beyond the understanding of the common people. Jesus brushed much of the Oral Law aside and gave two rules to his followers: to love God and to love their neighbour.

The Pharisees

The Pharisees were a sect who prided themselves that they kept the Oral Law down to the last detail. Many of them, as we shall see, made a big show of keeping the Sabbath laws, of fasting twice a week and of ceremonial washing after contact with Gentiles and other unclean objects. For the Pharisees the study and keeping of the Oral Law was religion and when Messiah came they believed that he would recognise them alone as the true people of God. Many of the Scribes, no doubt, where also Pharisees. The Pharisees, therefore, had a tendency to self-righteousness, and they appeared rather to despise other people, especially outcasts (tax-collectors, prostitutes) and all Gentiles.

The Sadducees   These were priests and the aristocrats of Jewry. The High Priest was at their head, and they performed the daily sacrifices in the Temple in Jerusalem, which was, in fact, a magnificent building and the largest known sanctuary in the world. This sect was virtually a 'closed shop', restricted to certain families. They derived a large income from the Temple poll tax (equivalent to a working man's wage for one day), the profits of money changers and from the sale of animals for sacrifice. They did not believe in an active after-life, nor in angels nor in the religious observances laid down by the Oral Law.

The Zealots   These comprised a Jewish underground movement in revolt against Rome. Many of them lived as outlaws and harried the Romans by surprise attack from the lonely hill country where they lived. One of them became a disciple of Jesus.
    An inner group was called, significantly, 'the Assassins'. Barabbas may have belonged to this group.

The coming of Christ
    On the surface, life under the Romans was good. Law and order were preserved and a reasonable standard of living maintained. Life in the towns was much in advance of the country. Antioch, for example, ('where the disciples were first called "Christian"') had two and a half miles of streets paved with marble and flanked by colonnades. It had a racecourse, theatres, temples, baths, fountains and a complete system of night lighting. There were flats five storeys high and in the more expensive houses, under-floor heating, libraries, picture galleries and fine mosaic work.
    The countryside, of course, was poor, and the poorest dwellings were built of mud and wood and had only one room. A flat roof would provide a second one for most of the year. The Jews were a hardworking, intelligent people and in Palestine there was no wide-spread destitution as there is in some parts of the world today.
    Yet there was an atmosphere of uncertainty and fear in the Empire. Those who governed kept their power by violence and intrigue. Either you murdered your rivals or they murdered you.
    Cruelty was commonplace and there was little respect for human life. Every Roman holiday provided its gladiatorial show where men and animals were forced to kill one another, and you

were lucky indeed if the entertainment contained special features such as a victim crucified and then, half dead, torn limb from limb by wild beasts.

But behind this cruel gaiety lurked a constant fear. How long could the good life continue? There were always wars and rumours of wars and everyone knew about the barbarians, those savage tribes outside the Empire, forever battering at its defences. Rome had strong armies, but were they unbeatable? Few people were convinced that they were and there was little hope for the future.

Religion provided none. Many people had lost their faith in the ancient gods and no longer visited the temples. They felt that the sacrifice of animals to the gods was useless and wasteful. They turned wistfully elsewhere for something new.

Teachers, visionaries and philosophers arose to meet the need but none, in the end, succeeded. Some people turned to Judaism as the most reasonable faith, but found the Jews themselves proud and exclusive.

The coming of Christ, then, was particularly suited to this time. His message of God's concern for all men travelled fast along the Roman roads, captured the imagination of men everywhere, so that when the official persecution of Christians ceased, it was discovered that nearly twenty per cent of the inhabitants of the Empire had already been converted.

Questions for revision

1. Compare the three provinces of Palestine with which Jesus was concerned. Why do you think he spent most of his public life in Galilee, seldom passed through Samaria, and when in Judaea spent more time in argument than he did in teaching?
2. Say what you know about life in Palestine under the Romans. Why did Christianity spread like 'a rushing, mighty wind' through the Empire?
3. Outline the chief characteristics of a. the Scribes, b. the Pharisees, c. the Sadducees, d. The Zealots.

The Four Gospels and their Writers

In nineteen hundred years the story of Christianity has spread through the world until today nearly a thousand million people claim Christianity as their religion. We can understand, therefore, that the four gospels, the record of Christ's life, have been subject to keen examination and criticism by both believers and unbelievers for many centuries. Who wrote them and how true are they?

They have survived this critical examination very well. 'Heaven and earth', said Jesus, 'shall pass away but my words shall not pass away.' This, we have good reason to believe, is true. From Christ's daily teaching of his disciples, from the early years when his extraordinary words and deeds were vividly recalled and taught and then commited to writing (see Luke **1**, 1-4) there have emerged these four records. They are not identical. In describing many incidents you will find that the writers vary, but that is what we should expect. Witnesses in giving evidence often differ on minor points of fact. But basically we have here the story of what Christ said and did, and as J.B. Phillips, the translator, says, the records have 'a ring of truth' about them.

How they came to be recorded is another question as we shall see when we read about the Synoptic Problem. Here we are mainly concerned with the traditional authors, Matthew, Mark, Luke and John, and what special reasons they would have for recording Christ's life.

Mark

John Mark, the author by tradition of this gospel, was the son of a certain Mary who lived in Jerusalem. She was a friend of Peter who returned to her house after his escape from prison (Acts **12**, 12). Mark made missionary journeys with Paul and Barnabas, and later joined Paul in Rome. He is said to have taken Christianity to Alexandria and died there a martyr.

His gospel was written under the influence of Peter and recounts a number of incidents in which Peter was specially involved (**1**, 16; **8**, 29; **9**, 5; **14**, 66-72; **16**, 7). It is therefore fresh and vivid in character, recording little details of how Christ acted as would be remembered by an eye-witness, for example:

Feeding of the five thousand, **6**, 39. They sat in companies of one hundred or fifty on the green grass.

Healing of the withered hand, **3, 5**. He looks round at the Pharisees with anger.

The storm, **4, 38**. Jesus is asleep on a cushion.

Jairus's daughter, **5, 41**. Jesus takes her by the hand.

Who will be the greatest, **9, 36**. Jesus takes a child, puts him in the middle of the group and takes him in his arms.

Blessing the children, **10, 16**. Jesus takes the children in the crook of his arm.

The rich young ruler, **10, 21**. Jesus looks at him with affection.

On the way to Jerusalem, **10, 32**. Jesus striding ahead of his disciples.

Notice also Mark's bluntness and candour: Jesus is unable to do any mighty works in Nazareth, **6, 5**; he is often moved with pity; he is amazed at their unbelief, **6, 6**; he is indignant with his disciples **10, 14**.

The gospel shows signs of having been written in haste and was probably designed for Christians in Rome who were suffering great persecution.

Luke

Luke wrote an account of Christianity from the birth of Jesus to the arrival of the Good News in Rome, the capital of the Gentile world. It is in two volumes: I Luke; II Acts.

Luke was a Gentile, a doctor (Col. **4**, 14) and tradition says that he was also an artist and painted a portrait of Mary, the mother of Jesus. He was a friend of Saint Paul, accompanying him on his second and third missionary journeys, and a companion during his imprisionment in Rome. He was not an eye-witness of Christ's ministry.

He had great literary ability. Renan, the French writer and critic, said that St Luke's gospel was 'the most beautiful book in the world'. Luke took great pains not only with his style of writing but in collecting his material and recording as exactly as possible the facts of Christ's life, as is evident from his introduction at the beginning of the gospel.

He wrote to convert Gentiles, for he emphasises the details which show Jesus to be the Saviour of all men rather than the Messiah of the Jews. He lays stress on Christ's interest and faith in Gentiles. Note in this connection:

1. He traces the genealogy of Christ to Adam, not Abraham.
2. He uses non-Jewish words such as master and lawyer, rather than the Jewish rabbi and scribe.

3. For dating purposes he uses the names of Roman emperors and officials as well as Jewish leaders (2, 1; 3, 1).
4. He brings out the virtues of Gentiles (his talk in the Nazareth synagogue, the ten lepers, the centurion, the good Samaritan).
5. He is the only writer to record the sending out of the Seventy (the supposed number of all nations).
6. He uses such expressions as, 'A light to lighten the Gentiles', 'All flesh shall see the salvation of God'.

Note also Luke's great interest in the poor and outcast: the shepherds at the birth (2, 8); the prostitute (7, 37); the great banquet (14, 16); the beggar Lazarus (16, 20); a despised tax-collector (19, 2); the penitent thief (23, 40).

In Luke also the importance of women and Christ's concern for them is stressed (the word 'woman' appears forty-three times); e.g. Elizabeth, Mary, Anna, the woman who was a prostitute, the widow of Nain, Mary and Martha, the women who accompanied the disciples and the women at the cross and at the tomb.

He also emphasises Christ's dependence on prayer: at his baptism, before choosing the twelve apostles, at Caesarea Philippi, the Transfiguration, in Gethsemane and on the cross. In three of Luke's recorded parables Jesus teaches the need for persistency and humility in prayer.

Finally, we should notice the frequency with which reference is made to the work of the Holy Spirit: in the life of John the Baptist and his parents, Simeon and Anna in the Temple, and in Christ's life at his conception, baptism, in the wilderness, after the mission of the Seventy, and the promise of the Spirit to his disciples before his ascension.

Matthew

Matthew, to whom this gospel is ascribed, was a tax-collector, Levi by name, whom Jesus called to be an apostle (9, 9). He wrote especially to convert Jews and unlike Luke, emphasises the Jewish character of Jesus.

He is constantly quoting the Jewish scriptures to prove that Jesus is Messiah:
Matthew, 1, 23. 'Behold a virgin shall conceive', Isaiah,
Matthew, 2, 6. 'And you, O Bethlehem', Jeremiah,
Matthew, 2, 15. 'Out of Egypt have I called my son. . .' Hosea,
Matthew, 2, 18. 'A voice was heard in Ramah. . .' Jeremiah,
Matthew, 2, 23. 'He shall be called a Nazarene. . .' Isaiah,
Matthew, 4, 15. 'The land of Zebulun. . .' Isaiah,

Matthew, **8**, 17. 'He took our infirmities. . .' Isaiah,

Matthew, **12**, 18. 'Behold my servant. . .' Isaiah,

Matthew, **13**, 35. 'I will open my mouth in parables. . .' Psalms,

Matthew, **21**, 5. 'Tell the daughter of Zion. . .' Isaiah,

Matthew, **27**, 9. 'And they took the thirty pieces of silver. . .' Jeremiah.

As a good Jew he avoids using the divine name and refers to the Kingdom of God as the Kingdom of Heaven.

He gives prominence to the Jewish Law (cf., Matt. **5, 6, 7**) and Jesus's right as Messiah to transcend it where necessary.

He declares Jesus to be the son of David and Abraham (**1**, 1) and his genealogy traces Jesus back to Abraham, the father of the Jewish race.

When he sends out the Twelve Apostles Matthew emphasises that they are sent only to the Jews, nor does he record Jesus going outside Jewish territory.

The gospel is very critical of the Jewish leaders and this would probably help converted Jews who were bitterly attacked to defend themselves against their own people.

The Fourth Gospel John, by tradition the writer of this gospel, was an apostle. His brother was James, his father, Zebedee. They were apparently a well-to-do family; his father had hired servants and knew the High Priest personally (see the Trial Scene). His mother, Salome, seems to have been the sister of the Virgin Mary. He was a disciple of John the Baptist before he was called by Christ. He was 'the disciple whom Jesus loved' (he never refers to himself by name in the gospel) and to whom Jesus commended Mary his mother, when he was on the cross.

His gospel is much different from the other three and was written later. The main factual differences are:

John	Synoptics
1. Written after A.D. 90*.	Written before A.D. 90.
2. Jesus makes several visits to Jerusalem.	Jesus's main ministry in Galilee emphasised.
3. Teaching mainly by long talks and arguments.	Teaching mainly by parables.
4. Messiahship constantly argued with rabbis.	Messiahship hardly mentioned.

* Some authorities, however, are now suggesting that the date is earlier than A.D. 90.

Note especially these passages where John adds to the synoptic accounts:

1. The incarnation **1**, 1-14. The Word made flesh.
2. The call of the disciples **1**, 29-51. Their association with John the Baptist.
3. Nicodemus **3**, 1-21 being born again.
4. Feeding of the five thousand **6**, 25-59.
5. The disciples will not desert him, **6**, 60-71 (cf., Caesarea Philippi).
6. 'I am the good shepherd', **10**, 1-18.
7. After the last supper: the gift of the Holy Spirit, **14**, 15-17, 26, **16**, 7-14; the true vine, **15**, 1-8.

Four additional features distinguish this gospel from the synoptics:

1. There are only eight miracles recorded in this gospel (see the list on p. 81) and they are referred to as 'signs' - signs of God's power revealed in Christ, indicating who and what he was, the Messiah. This view of Christ's miraculous power is similar to that expressed in Luke **7**, 18-23 and Matthew **11**, 2-6 where proof of Christ's messiahship is given to John the Baptist. Jesus refused the Pharisees any other sign of his unique personality.
2. In place of the synoptic terms 'Kingdom of God' or 'Kingdom of Heaven' John uses the term 'Eternal Life', though the terms are used interchangeably in Mark's account of the rich young ruler (**10**, 17-31). The word 'life' has great prominence in the Fourth Gospel. 'I came,' said Jesus, 'that they might have life and have it more abundantly' (**10**, 10). Those who receive him have eternal life and such, according to the Synoptics, are already in the Kingdom of God.
3. John is well-known for his famous 'I am. . .' passages:
   'I am the bread of life. . . ,' **6**, 35.
   'I am the light of the world. . . ,' **8**, 12; **9**, 5.
   'I am the resurrection and the life. . . ,' **11**, 25.
   'I am the door' (of the sheepfold), **10**, 7.
   'I am the good shepherd,' **10**, 11, 14.
   'I am the way, the truth and the life,' **14**, 6.
   'I am the true vine,' **15**, 1.

The first three sayings should be studied in conjunction with the particular miracles with which they are closely linked.

4. John emphasises more than any other gospel, Christ's relationships with individuals. No less than twenty-seven personal

interviews, of varying length, are recorded in the gospel. For instance, we find a closer personal relationship between Jesus and Pilate in John's gospel than in the Synoptics.

Questions for revision

1. What do we know of the lives of Matthew, Mark and Luke? How are their characters reflected in the gospels named after them?
2. Summarise the main differences between the Fourth Gospel and the other three. What do we know about the apostle John?

The Synoptic Problem

The first three gospels are quite different from the Fourth Gospel, (see p. 10). They are known as the Synoptic Gospels - 'synoptic' meaning seen from the same view point. They are similar to one another in content and sometimes in the order of the events described. For example, Mark contains 661 verses, and out of these no fewer than 606 are found in either Luke or Matthew in similar form. Compare the Healing of the Leper in Matt. 8, 1-4, Mark 1, 40-45 and Luke 5, 12-16.

How is this similarity to be accounted for? This is the synoptic problem about which there has been considerable argument for many years. Below in brief and simplified form are outlines of three possible explanations.

1. The oral tradition

In a community having very few books, the human memory is trained and used to a remarkable extent. (cf., Muslim countries where children of nine can recite the whole of the Koran.) The incidents in the life of Christ, his parables and teaching were readily and accurately committed to memory by eye-witnesses and passed on, sometimes in written form, from one body of Christians to another. This body of teaching is known as the oral tradition. Thus, writing independently of one another, Mark, Luke and Matthew (who was himself an eye-witness), may each have drawn on this oral tradition. (Note that this is the Christian oral tradition and has no connection with the Pharisees Oral Law or Tradition of the Elders mentioned on p. 4).

This view is supported by the statements of early Church leaders such as Papias and Irenaeus but it does not appear to account sufficiently for the word for word resemblances in the gospels.

2. Mutual interdependence

This theory is that one gospel writer simply copied from another. This is unlikely because (a) the writers would hardly wish to do this, (b) if they had done so, the order of events described would be more similar than it is, (c) all the really important material would have been recorded in each gospel, which it is not.

3. The Documentary Theory

Mark is generally agreed to be the first of the four gospels to be written. The Documentary Theory is that Matthew and Luke had Mark's gospel before them plus another document, now lost, and called for convenience Q (German *quelle* - source) containing the sayings of Christ. It would contain over 200 verses common to Luke and Matthew which are not found in Mark. Some scholars now think that Q may have consisted of more than one document.

Canon Streeter suggested a variation of this theory: that there were four documents available: L, Q, M and Mark.

L (Proto-Luke) which was compiled by Luke perhaps from travel notes or by someone else. This with Mark plus Q was available to Luke when he wrote the gospel we have today.

M an oral or written source, possibly containing the Sermon on the Mount, which Matthew used together with Mark and Q.

The main weaknesses of this theory are (a) that no trace of these documents (L, Q, M) has ever been found; (b) that no allowance is made for the fact that Mark, Matthew and Luke could very well have known one another (Mark and Luke are mentioned as possibly together in Col. 4, 10, 14 and II Timothy 4, 11) and that they could have met and conferred on several occasions and shared their knowledge, each emphasising what he felt to be important in his own gospel.

Nevertheless, scholars consider a solution along the lines of this Documentary Theory the most acceptable and are still discussing it.

Questions for revision

What is the Synoptic Problem and what solution to it does the Documentary Theory offer?

Birth and Boyhood

The only stories of Christ's infancy are found in Matthew and Luke. They seem to have been selected according to the purpose of the writers: Matthew writes to impress the Jews and therefore includes the story of King Herod and the distinguished visitors from the East; Luke, wanting always to show Christ's concern for common people everywhere, stresses the humble circumstances of Christ's birth and includes the story of the shepherds.

Luke's introduction
Luke 1, 1-4
Compare these verses with Luke's introduction to his second book, The Acts of the Apostles. In these two books he tells the story of the Gospel (good news) from Christ's birth in Bethlehem to the Gospel's arrival at the heart of the Gentile Empire, Rome. He speaks of the many records he has consulted which may have included Mark and possibly Q, and he claims to give an orderly and accurate account of what actually took place. His friend, Theophilus, is unknown, but the name, meaning 'Lover of God', may be a pseudonym for a high Roman official.

Zechariah in the Temple
Luke 1, 5-25
The remarkable vision Zechariah had in the Temple and the strange circumstances of John the Baptist's birth emphasise the unique importance of Christ's coming. He is to be preceded by a great prophet - a second Elijah - to prepare people for his arrival.

In Christ's day there were 20,000 priests in Palestine. No priest would be elected twice in his lifetime to burn incense in the Temple. It was therefore a memorable day for Zechariah. In white robes and with bare feet, on the striking of a bell, he threw incense on the altar fire.

Zechariah's delay in giving the blessing would certainly alarm the people, since it was believed that to be as near to God as was Zechariah was dangerous and could result in death (Lev. 16, 11-14).

Dumbness, or the inability to express oneself, is a well-known psychological result of a great shock. Barrenness, as in Elizabeth, was considered a great misfortune. The introduction of angels in this story is in line with a general belief, shared by Christ himself, that man was not the only spiritual being that God had created.

15

The Annunciation and visit to Elizabeth

Luke 1, 26-56

Matt. 1, 18-25

The Annunciation is the name given to the visit of the angel Gabriel to Mary announcing that she should have a son. His name is to be Jesus, meaning 'God and Saviour' and he will be 'the Son of the Most High', a special relationship with God not clearly defined. Notice the delicate way in which the conception of Jesus is announced.

Mary visits Elizabeth and, it seems, stays till the birth of John. The beautiful thanksgiving that Mary recites is known as the Magnificat.

Matt. 1, 18-25 is mainly concerned with Joseph's problem of Mary having a child other than by him. In normal circumstances, Joseph as a strict Jew, would be required to divorce her.

The birth of John the Baptist

Luke 1, 57-80

The writing tablet used by Zechariah would have a surface of soft wax written on with a metal stylus.

Zechariah's thanksgiving vv. 68-79 is known as the Benedictus. In vv. 72, 73 there is a reference to God's promises to Abraham, of which the Pharisees were very proud, as they referred to themselves as the Sons of Abraham. The promises are given and repeated in Gen. 12, 3; 17, 4; and 22, 16 and 17. (Compare John the Baptist's view, Luke 3, 8.)

John later lived in the wilderness. Many great religious leaders have prepared for their work in solitude, as did Jesus after his baptism.

The birth of Christ

Luke 2, 1-21

Matt. 2, 1.

In Egypt there was a census every fourteen years. This may have been so in Palestine. A census is known to have taken place in A.D. 6, so the one referred to here would be about 8 B.C. It would take some time as the Jewish custom was for each family to return to its birthplace. Thus Christ may well have been born about 6 B.C. He was almost certainly born before A.D. 1 and therefore our own dating is wrong. It was computed by a monk in the sixth century whose calculations are now generally acknowledged to be out by some years.

The season of Christ's birth is not known. December 25th has been celebrated since the fourth century.

The inn in Bethlehem would be an enclosed space with a lamp at the entrance gate. The stable would in any case be more private than the recesses round the courtyard used by travellers. Swaddling clothes were linen bands used to 'strengthen' the baby's limbs. The manger may have been a hollow in the ground.

Unlike the shepherds, Mary was not astonished, and apparently

kept silence in regard to these events until possibly after the
Resurrection.

Circumcision and the visit to the Temple

Luke 2, 21-40   The laws for purification and presentation are given in Lev. **12**.
Originally the eldest son was consecrated to God (cf. Hannah and
Samuel), but in Christ's day he was presented to God and then
'bought back' by the offer of an alternative sacrifice - doves or
pigeons by poor people. Note that young pigeons were more
easily caught than old ones.

Simeon and Anna, like Zechariah and Elizabeth, were deeply
religious and would expect a spiritual leader rather than a militant
Messiah.

The words of Simeon, 'Now lettest thou thy servant. . .' are
known as the Nunc Dimittis (the Latin for the introductory words)
and have been used in Christian churches since the 5th century.

The words in vv. 34 and 35 are prophetic. Jesus was certainly
'spoken against', being called by his enemies the Deceiver, the
Samaritan, 'the hung' and a demoniac. Pagans charged Christians
with cannibalism and other atrocities. The sword piercing Mary's
soul would be the spectacle of the Crucifixion.

The Wise Men

Matt. 2   Astrology was much studied in the east. In Persia, the wise men,
or magi, studied the stars with great interest.

In the seventeenth century, the astronomer Kepler found that
Saturn, Jupiter and Mars came into conjunction between 1603
and 1606. A new star then appeared between Mars and Saturn,
shone brilliantly for one year and disappeared. Kepler calculated
that this conjunction would happen only once in 800 years and
that it had happened in the year 7 B.C. just before Christ was born.

Gold, frankincense and myrrh were symbols of kingship, deity
and sorrow.

The cunning plot of Herod is in character with what is known
of him. Archelaus, whom Joseph rightly feared, was deposed for
cruelty in A.D. 6.

Comparison of birth stories

Matthew writing for the Jews gives many quotations from Old
Testament prophecy, for he wished that every event in Christ's
birth should be recognised as the fulfilment of prophecy. Note
also the use of dreams to direct people. In Matthew, Joseph is the
central figure. None of Matthew's stories is repeated in Luke.

Luke writing for Gentiles does not stress the Jewish prophecy in describing the birth. He tells the story of the shepherds for they were little better than outcasts, and continually implies that Jesus came to help such people. Christ is also 'a light to lighten the Gentiles'. Mary is the central figure in Luke's account.

Genealogies (family trees)

Luke **3**, 23-38
Matt. **1**, 1-17

Both lists trace Jesus's ancestry through Joseph because the Jews gave importance only to male descent. The names from David onwards differ.

Matthew's purpose was to trace Christ's descent through David to Abraham, the Father of the Jewish race. Luke's intention, as a writer mainly to the Gentiles, was to trace Christ back to Adam as the Father of the human race.

Neither list can claim to be accurate or complete.

Passover visit to Jerusalem

Luke2, 41-52

Jesus was now twelve and he would be receiving instruction in the Jewish law from the local rabbi. He would then read the scriptures at a service in the local synagogue and in the eyes of the Jewish congregation become a man, a Son of the Law. His presence at any service would count towards the twelve males necessarily present before a service could begin. Today the ceremony takes place at the age of thirteen.

In Exodus **23**, 14-17 it is stated that male Jews should go to Jerusalem for Passover, Pentecost and the Feast of Tabernacles. This was too much for many Jews but most in Palestine tried to go at least once a year.

The Feast of the Passover coincides roughly with the Christian Easter and the reaping of the harvest in Palestine. It commemorates the deliverance of the Israelites from Egypt and is celebrated in every Jewish home.

Jesus is surprised that his parents did not look for him first in the Temple. The things concerning his Father and his Father's house, the Temple, had always been most important in his life.

Questions for revision

1. Describe the visit of the Wise Men to Palestine and the effect that they had on King Herod. What other visitors, according to Luke, did Jesus have?
2. Describe the events which lead up to the birth and naming of John the Baptist.

Preparation for the Ministry

Baptism and teaching of John the Baptist
Mark **1**, 1-8
Matt. **3**, 1-12   *The prophets*
Luke **3**, 1-18   There is a strange and important fact about the Israelites that
applies to no other nation. During their long history, whenever
they or their rulers did wrong, a holy man or prophet often
appeared in order to denounce their sin and direct them to live
according to God's commandments. You will have heard of some
of these famous prophets: Samuel, Elijah, Elisha and later, the
prophets who wrote down their message, such as Isaiah and
Jeremiah.

But for nearly four centuries no famous prophet had been
heard in Israel. Then John the Baptist appeared. You can well
imagine the great stir it caused throughout the nation especially
when people listened to strange stories about his appearance and
message.

John the Baptist
He was a stern, hard man, living the life of a hermit. It is likely
that he was an orphan early in life and like others who felt the
hopelessness of the times, he 'contracted out' of society and went
to live in the desert. This particular desert, the Wilderness of
Judaea, was an appalling desolation running down to the shores
of the Dead Sea and known as The Horror.

Notice John's spartan dress and food as described in Matthew
and Luke. Locusts, large grasshopper-like insects, are still eaten.
You remove their heads, legs and wings and boil them in water or
fry them in fat.

His message
John's message was frightening. Messiah - the deliverer - was about
to appear and immediately there would be a terrible judgement.
As a farmer separates the wheat from the chaff, Messiah would
separate the good from the wicked, and the wicked like the chaff
would suffer the agony of being burnt up and destroyed. (Note
that Jesus did not behave in this way - he wished to save the
wicked, not to destroy them.)

Therefore, said John, everyone must immediately be baptised as a sign of repentance for his sin. It was simply no use their saying, 'We are the Sons of Abraham' - God's chosen people. It was the kind of life they led that mattered.

In Luke we are told that John gave special directions:

1. To the *people*, to be generous, kind and share their food and clothing with the poor.
2. To the *publicans*, to be honest.
3. To the *soldiers*, not to abuse their power and to be content with their wages.

Among the great crowds that flocked to see John some thought that he was Messiah. 'No, I am not,' he replied. 'I am not fit to unfasten his shoes. I baptise you with water; he will baptise you with the Holy Spirit.'

The Baptism of Jesus
Mark 1, 9-11
Matt. 3, 13-17
Luke 3, 21, 22

This was a vital experience for Jesus. At his baptism, he exchanged the quiet, comfortable life of a village carpenter for a turbulent public career in which he was both loved and hated, surrounded at times by men who would gladly have murdered him, at others by adoring crowds who would joyfully have crowned him.

After his baptism Jesus was immediately aware of the Holy Spirit descending like a dove upon him and the voice of God acknowledging him as His son. (N.B. two other occasions when Jesus heard a voice: the Transfiguration Mark 9, 7 and during the week in which he died John 12, 28.)

Why did Jesus accept a baptism of repentance? In Matthew John protests that Jesus ought baptise him. Possibly, in addition to this being a decisive step in his life, Jesus also wanted to give public support to John's work.

John in prison
Luke 3, 19, 20.

Though many lawyers and Pharisees among the Jews were very ready to denounce adultery as being against the Law and even meriting the death penalty, no-one but John had the courage to denounce Herod Antipas for his adulterous marriage to his half-brother Philip's wife. John now paid for his boldness by imprisonment. He was shut up in the fortress of Machor whose ruins still stand on a desolate spot north of the Dead Sea.

The Temptation
Mark 1, 12-13
Matt. 4, 1-11
Luke 4, 1-13

The record of Christ's temptations can have come only from Christ himself. Like us all he was tempted throughout his life but especially at this point when he was now fully aware of his calling and of his great powers. How was he to use them? What had

John prophesied about him and what did the people expect of the Messiah? In the solitude of the wilderness he struggled against the temptations to use his powers to benefit himself or to be a a popular, conquering Messiah (a second David).

Jesus always spoke of the devil as a person - an active, evil spirit, constantly at hand tempting us to do wrong. 'Broad is the way,' he said, 'that leads to destruction and many there be that take it.'

Luke says that for forty days he ate nothing. This may imply, as in Matthew, that he observed the laws of fasting, which would not deprive him of all food. It is a known fact that fasting does help the mind to reason very clearly.

Stones into bread

The temptation to turn a stone into bread would not be easy to resist. The small flat circular stones that lie about in this wilderness would be the shape and size of the loaves he was used to seeing made at home. Possibly it was a symbolic temptation to overcome personal difficulties - hunger, thirst, tiredness and the aches and pains of daily life. But Jesus never used his miraculous powers to help himself. In this way, he retained his ordinary human nature and remained an example that we could follow. Jesus in reply to this temptation asserts that man needs not only material things but also the guidance of God to fulfil his life on earth.

World conqueror

The devil then in his imagination shows him 'all the kingdoms of the earth' - at that time this would mean the Roman Empire. To bow down to the devil here would be to use evil means - force and oppression - to become a world conqueror. To see the Romans cast out of their land and to see themselves as the leading nation on earth would delight the vast majority of Jews in Christ's day. They expected Messiah to be a second David. But Christ would not use force. Note:

1. His attitude to the disciples who wished to burn the Samaritan villages (Luke 9, 51-56).
2. His refusal to be made King after the feeding of the five thousand (John 6, 15).
3. His displeasure with Peter when he cut off the ear of the High Priest's servant (Matt. 26, 52).

To win by magic

The third temptation (Matthew puts it second) was to descend from the parapet of the Temple. In reply to Jews who asked where Messiah, when he came, would first be seen, rabbis used to say, 'Descending from the highest point on the holiest building in the holiest of cities'   the Temple in Jerusalem. The temptation was, therefore, to astound the people by magic and to win an easy victory (or a bloody revolution). The Pharisees were always badgering him to give them 'a sign' that he was Messiah. Jesus's proof of his messiahship was quite different. Note his answer to John the Baptist's messengers (Luke 7, 22).

Christ chooses his first disciples

Mark 1, 14-20
Matt. 4, 12-25
Luke 5, 1-11

The four men, Simon, Andrew, James and John whom Jesus made his disciples, had quite possibly already met him (John 1, 35-42). In Luke's account the call of the disciples is preceded by a miracle - the miraculous catch of fish. Christ's first thought after speaking to the crowd was for his disappointed followers. Notice Simon's strange reaction to the miracle; it gives a ring of truth to the story. In Matthew we have another prophecy quoted - this time accounting for Christ settling in Capernaum.

Christ rejected at Nazareth

Mark 6, 1-6
Matt. 13, 53-58
Luke 4, 14-30

Jesus returning to his home town would be a rather distinguished visitor and naturally would be asked by the local rabbi to speak at the synagogue service. As was the custom he would stand to read the scriptures, possibly translating them from Hebrew into Aramaic. Then he would sit to address the congregation.

The longest account is given in Luke. It seems that the congregation's anger arose from three causes:
1. The carpenter's son was claiming to be Messiah, for the passage he read from Isaiah would be recognised as a description of Messiah.
2. He would not work any miracles in Nazareth.
3. He showed that Old Testament prophets thought that Gentiles were sometimes more worthy of their help than were the Jews.

The punishment for blasphemy was stoning, and throwing Christ over the cliff edge was a form of it. Notice Christ's mysterious majesty in walking away (also seen when he cleansed the Temple and before the soldiers in Gethsemane).

It is possible that Christ made two separate visits to his home town. Both Matthew's and Mark's versions suggest that the visit was made with his disciples in the course of his general ministry, whereas Luke's very full description suggests that he was alone and that the visit took place soon after his temptation in the wilderness.

If there were, in fact, two visits, the results of them seem to have been the same.

Questions for revision

1. Describe   (a)   the kind of man John the Baptist was;
       (b)   his message and work on the banks of the River Jordan;
       (c)   what happened when Jesus met him there.
2. Write a full account of what happened in the wilderness when Jesus was tempted by the devil. Why was Jesus tempted, do you think, immediately after his baptism?
3. Describe Jesus's return to Nazareth and what was the consequence of it. Why did the people want to kill him?

The Ministry

Capernaum

It is possible that Jesus had some thoughts of making Nazareth the centre of his work, at least in the early part of his ministry, but the open hostility he met there had made the idea impracticable. Instead, he made Capernaum his centre. Unlike Nazareth, this was a town of great importance. It lay on the shores of the Sea of Galilee and did much business in fishing and agriculture. It was large enough to be called a city; it had a Roman garrison and a customs house.

Jesus is referred to here on occasion as being 'at home'. What was this home? Peter's possibly; or if Joseph was now dead - and we hear nothing of him after Christ's boyhood - Jesus could well have built a house for his mother here. The term 'carpenter' would also include stonemason.

The cure of the demoniac

Mark **1**, 21-28
Luke **4**, 31-37

Christ's reception in the synagogue in Capernaum was much more friendly than in Nazareth. The local rabbi apparently invited him to speak and the people heard him gladly. They were impressed by two things in particular:
1. The authority and ease with which Christ spoke. The Scribes who normally taught used the Oral Law for constant reference which was so complicated that it became a burden to the people.
2. His ability to drive out an unclean spirit.
Evil spirits were generally held responsible for mental derangement. If Jesus had other views he did not voice them. He always spoke as if evil were a terrible force in men's lives, affecting them both mentally and physically.

Christ cures Peter's mother-in-law and others

Mark **1**, 29-34
Matt. **8**, 14-17
Luke **4**, 38-41

Notice Mark's description: 'He took her by the hand' - the kind of detail that Peter, as an eyewitness would remember. Notice also that the crowds waited till sunset, the end of the Sabbath, before bringing their relatives and friends for healing.

Christ's popularity

Mark **1**, 35-39
Luke **4**, 42-44

Overwhelmed by the large crowds which came to him, Christ finds refuge in prayer in the early morning. He decides to take the gospel further afield.

Healing a leper

Mark 1, 40-45

Luke 5, 12-16

Matt. 8, 1-4

To the Pharisees and lawyers leprosy appeared a hopeless disease, as indeed it was, up to recent times. They said, therefore, that it was 'the finger of God' upon a man, meaning that God, for some reason - possibly some sin - had afflicted a man with leprosy and nothing could be done about it. A leper must leave his home town and must not come within a certain distance of the town walls. He must behave as a mourner with rent clothes, dishevelled hair and the lower part of his face covered. One rabbi boasted that he always threw stones at lepers to keep them at a distance. It seems that everyone was terrified of catching the disease.

Jesus's attitude was completely the reverse of this. He seems to say that it is not God's wish that anyone should suffer in this way and he is always anxious to effect a cure. 'If I by the finger of God cast out the demons, then is the Kingdom of God come among you,' he said. He broke the laws (touching the leper) in order to heal the man.

Notice the strict instructions. He commanded him:
1. To go away immediately.
2. To tell nobody what happened to him.
3. To show himself to a priest to get a written bill of health.
4. To offer thanksgiving sacrifices.

The enormous crowds that were following Jesus explain why he commanded the leper to tell no one. But it was too much for the leper to remain silent.

The paralytic and the forgiving of sins

Mark 2, 1-12

Matt. 9, 1-8

Luke 5, 17-26

It is likely that the house - possibly Peter's house - where Jesus performed this miracle flanked a courtyard on three sides. This would have made it impossible for the men carrying their sick friend to approach Jesus through this packed enclosure.

They therefore mounted the exterior stone steps on to the roof. Roofs were flat and provided an extra 'room' for prayer and relaxation. They had a palisade, which according to Mosaic law had to be one metre high. As the roof would consist of earth mixed with stone and beaten hard, it is likely that they removed the loose tiles that would cover the verandah.

Jesus in first forgiving the man's sins may have felt that his mental state was directly connected with his physical illness. Compare John 5, 14 the man cured by the sheep pool.

Jesus uses the title 'Son of Man' on many occasions to describe himself, especially when he was forecasting his own sufferings. In Psalm 8 and in Ezekiel it means 'man'; in Daniel it means the representative of faithful Israel. In other sacred Jewish writings it means a supernatural being. At this stage in his life for Jesus to use the term 'Messiah' would have been disastrous, whereas 'Son of Man' would leave his hearers puzzling.

The call of Matthew
Mark **2**, 13-22
Matt. **9**, 9-17
Luke **5**, 27-39

The tax office in Capernaum lay at the junction of the roads leading to Tyre, Damascus and Jerusalem.

Levi, who as a disciple is known by the name Matthew, was doubly hated by patriotic Jews: he collected taxes for the occupying power, and with other tax-collectors had a reputation for extortion and fraud (compare Zaccheus, Luke **19**, 1-10) and as a Jew he betrayed his country by working for the Romans.

Not only were great numbers of respectable people rather disgusted by the sight of Jesus and his disciples having a good time with Levi and other shady characters, but they also noticed that neither Jesus nor his disciples observed days of fasting. The Pharisees made a great fuss of fasting, the strictest of them fasting on Thursdays and Mondays in commemoration of Moses' ascent of Mount Sinai and his return. Some of them even put ash on their faces to impress people with their suffering. When they criticised Jesus for not fasting he replied that he was the bridegroom and that his disciples might fast after he had left them.

Jewish teachers often likened God to the bridegroom and the Jewish people to his bride. When Messiah came it would be like a marriage feast, for God would then be present in his kingdom on earth.

The reference to the wine not being put into old bottles may mean that Jesus does not see how his new teaching can possibly be confined to the old rigid forms of Judaism. Because of this he is meeting increasing opposition from the lawyers and Pharisees.

New wine as it ferments stretches the skin of the wine bottle. New wine put into an old bottle with its skin already stretched would tend to burst the bottle.

The disciples pluck the corn
Mark **2**, 23-28
Matt. **12**, 1-8
Luke **6**, 1-5

To reap and thresh corn on the Sabbath was to work unnecessarily and was therefore breaking the Law. The quantity - a million ears of corn or merely one - did not matter. Jesus breaks the Law regularly in order to help and relieve people from pain and worry; here he justified it because breaking it certainly does nobody any harm.

26

The disciples may have been in need of food as seems likely from Christ's description of their Jewish hero, David, desecrating the special bread, consecrated to God. This was the Bread of the Presence, twelve loaves, placed in the Holy Shrine, to be eaten only by the priests.

Christ says that the Sabbath was made for man's benefit, not man for the Sabbath's. Some pious Jews even argued that God created man in order to have someone to keep the Sabbath. To say that he, the Son of Man, was lord of the Sabbath, was to put himself once again in the place of God, which again was blasphemy in the eyes of the Pharisees.

The man with the withered hand

Mark **3**, 1-6	Notice the hard, unfeeling attitude of the Pharisees. They watched
Matt. **12**, 9-21	Jesus with hostility. This is the meaning of the Greek verb here.
Luke **6**, 6-11	The man with the withered hand meant nothing to them; their

Sabbath laws came always before human need. This really angered Jesus and he silenced them in front of the whole congregation. The Herodians were a political party supporting Herod and were normally opposed to the Pharisees. See also Mark **12**, 13-17.

Jesus retires and chooses his twelve companions

Mark **3**, 7-19	Christ had by now made the Pharisees and lawyers very hostile.
Matt. **10**, 2-4	Twice in their eyes he had been guilty of blasphemy: forgiving sins
Luke **6**, 12-19	and calling himself lord of the Sabbath. He had upheld the breaking

of the Sabbath laws: in the cornfield and again in the synagogue. He had touched a leper. He had taken a tax-collector as a disciple and had feasted with other undesirable people in Matthew's house. And, in addition, he had made the Pharisees look rather small in the eyes of the people. No wonder they began to scheme how they could destroy him.

For a time Jesus retired from this hotbed of hostility and was found somewhere by the sea of Galilee. But still the crowds pressed upon him, so that the disciples kept a boat ready in case they became too great for him.

Luke tells us that, in contrast, before Jesus chose his twelve companions, he spent a whole night in prayer.

Amongst them, by far the most important was Simon Peter, who later after Christ's ascension was to become leader of the apostles. Peter was a fisherman from Bethsaida. Later with his wife and mother-in-law he had his home in Capernaum, where it seems that Jesus stayed from time to time. He acted often as spokesman of the Twelve. He was at first impulsive and unreliable. Notice specially what he says on important occasions (e.g. Caesarea Philippi Matt. **16**, 17, 18; The Transfiguration Matt. **17**, 4; When Christ decides to go to Jerusalem Matt. **16**, 22; The Last Supper Luke **22**, 33; Gethsemane John **18**, 10; Christ's trial Mark **14**, 66-72; After the Resurrection John **21**, 15-22).

John, who by tradition was later responsible for the Fourth Gospel and the book of Revelation, was specially beloved by Christ. Simon the Zealot had belonged to the violent revolutionary party. Only Christ could have reconciled Simon the Zealot with Matthew, the tax-collector, who otherwise would have been the bitterest of enemies.

Healing the centurion's servant

Matt. **8** 5-13
Luke **7**, 1-10

The story has slight differences in the two gospels. In Matthew we are told that the centurion came to Jesus himself; in Luke, a deputation of Jewish elders came speaking very highly of the centurion.

A legion in the Roman army consisted of 6000 men, commanded by six tribunes. It was divided into ten cohorts, each cohort into three maniples and a maniple into two centuries. A centurion was in charge of a century - a hundred men.

This one, like many other Gentiles, had great respect for the Jewish faith but would feel that Jesus would not wish to enter a Gentile house. Thus, he likens Christ's power over the spiritual world to his own in the material world, and is sure Christ can heal his servant without seeing him. Christ is amazed at his faith. (Compare what Christ said in Nazareth about Elijah, Elisha and Gentiles Luke **4**, 24-27).

The widow of Nain's son

Luke **7**, 11-17

The town of Nain, forty kilometres south west of Capernaum, is identified with the modern village of Nein, approached by a rocky, narrow mountain path.

The body of the young man lying on a stretcher was being carried outside the town for burial. The widow Jesus would have great pity for, since both her husband and her only son were dead.

In touching the stretcher Jesus, as when he touched the leper, broke the Law and became unclean. This law, evidently, did not concern him when it was a matter of helping people. Christ's effect upon the crowd was to fill them with reverence and fear.

The two other incidents when Christ is recorded as raising the dead were Jairus's daughter and Lazarus.

The message from John the Baptist

Luke **7**, 18-35

Matt. **11**, 1-19

John was now in prison in Machor but was able to keep in touch with his friends.

His imprisonment had possibly begun to make him doubt. At Jordan he had preached that Messiah would come to judge mankind. If Jesus was indeed Messiah why should John still be languishing in prison? So he sent his messengers to find out the truth.

Jesus answered by showing them the work of healing that he was engaged in, and quoting from the Old Testament. He sent them back knowing that John would recognise that this too was what Messiah would do when he came.

After John's disciples had gone, Jesus defended John before the crowd which probably contained Pharisees who had bitterly opposed him. What should they have expected of a prophet in the desert? A weak fop of a man dressed in the style of a courtier? Of course, John would be hard and stern as a messenger of God calling for repentance. Yet the Pharisees behaved like spoilt children. Nothing would please them. John, a great prophet, they sneered at as a moody, melancholy hermit; Jesus, they condemned as a glutton and a drunkard because he was the opposite, sharing joyfully the life of the common people.

Great though John was, he was the last of the prophets before Christ. Since Christ there has been a new covenant with God and all those who enter on this covenant must have greater privileges and advantages than John.

Jesus, Simon and the sinful woman

Luke **7**, 36-

8, 3

This incident shows how many of the Pharisees regarded sinners, for the woman was most likely a prostitute, possibly Mary Magdalene.

This Pharisee, Simon, had treated Jesus with contempt in the way in which he had received him as Jesus, himself, pointed out. The woman made up for his failures. This was possible: (a) because it was customary among the rich to allow anyone to enter one's house and people would enter and watch a meal in progress; (b) the guests reclined on low divans around the table, having left their sandals at the door.

A rabbi would not normally eat with common people or speak

with a woman. He would expect a holy man or prophet to be filled with disgust by the woman and to repel her. (Compare the incident in John **8**, 3-11, where the Pharisees drag an adulterer before Christ.)

This is the second instance we have recorded of Christ forgiving sins.

The unforgiveable sin

Mark **3**, 20-35
Luke **11**, 14-32,
8, 19-21
Matt. **12**, 22-50

In Mark we are told that at this time his mother and brothers (or close relatives, if the tradition is accepted that Mary had Jesus only) were looking for him to take him home, as it was said that he was out of his mind. Later, the family seemed to show more understanding of his work (his brother, James, we are told became head of the church in Jerusalem.) But at this point, with Christ's constant journeyings, the enormous crowds which must have obscured what was going on and the constant denouncing of him by the rabbis to whom the family was bound to listen, we can understand their perplexity. His brief reply to them shows that the Kingdom of God is more important to him than even family ties.

In Luke and Matthew we have also a miracle recorded that astonished the people and enraged the Pharisees who can think of nothing better to say than that the healing work of Christ came directly from an evil spirit within him - Beelzebub. Beelzebub or Beelzebul was a pagan god, but in Christ's day the word, like 'Satan', meant 'the Prince of Devils'.

Beelzebub and the Holy Spirit

Jesus replies logically - and with much patience in view of this horrible accusation - that if Beelzebub does good he is defeating his own ends. Jesus reminds them that many Pharisees practice exorcism. Are they also inspired by the Prince of Devils? No, says Jesus. The evil and sickness in man is cast out by 'the finger of God' and the happiness that results is the happiness which everyone who is in God's kingdom feels.

Jesus then points out how wicked is this accusation against him. It represents the worst of all sins - the sin against the Holy Ghost. This is more an attitude - as with the Pharisees - than a single action. If men declare that good is evil and that God's spirit is the devil, they cannot be forgiven since it is only through God's spirit that they can find forgiveness. They condemn themselves.

In Matthew, he harshly condemns the Pharisees who made this accusation. 'You viper's brood! How can your words be good when you yourselves are evil?' He refuses them a sign: even the people of Nineveh and the Queen of Sheba showed more understanding of God than they did!

The wicked demon

In Matt. 12, 43 and Luke 11, 24 Jesus tells the parable of the grisly demon cast out of a man's mind and how it wanders over the desert and then returns with seven companions like itself. Christ's followers must be aware always of the terrible struggle of good and evil within man. It is not enough simply to cast out the evil in our minds; we must replace it with active goodness.

The parable of the sower

Mark 4, 1-20 26-29	The commonest definition of a parable is 'an earthly story with a heavenly meaning'. It is really a comparison.
Luke 8, 4-15 Matt. 13, 1-23	Jesus took everyday incidents for his stories, but each story had a parallel meaning in the spiritual world which, he taught, surrounds us and extends far beyond the narrow limits of this visible life.

Many of these parables were used to describe the Kingdom of Heaven - that perfect society in which men love God and one another.

This parable describes four ways in which people react to his teaching (the seed). The condition of their minds is represented by the depth and quality of soil that a sower would meet with: 1. non-existent soil, 2. thin and stony soil, 3. soil choked by thorns and 4. a good depth of soil. Notice the interesting reasons Jesus gives for why people reject his words: evil thoughts immediately replace them; they have no staying power against persecution; their worldly cares; the false glamour of wealth; all kinds of evil desires.

Why parables?

The reason Jesus gives for speaking in parables is perplexing and a number of explanations have been suggested. Here is a possible one: since his enemies have persisted in criticism and derision of his direct teaching, he now speaks in parables so that those in sympathy with his gospel will understand their meaning, and those who listen only to argue and find fault will hear little that they can criticise.

The short parable that follows in Mark alone (4, 26-29), the seed which grew secretly, suggests that once the seed (Christ's teaching)is sown, it oftens grows without any help from outside.

The stilling of the storm

Mark 4, 35-41
Matt. 8, 18, 23-27
Luke 8, 22-25

There are one or two occasions when Jesus seems to over-rule the known laws of nature in the external world. This is one of them (others are: The feeding of the five thousand; Walking on the sea). Sudden, violent squalls occur on the Sea of Galilee. They end often as suddenly as they come. Mark tells us that there were many other little boats accompanying Jesus and the disciples. Notice, as in the miraculous catch of fishes, that Christ's powers strike fear into the minds of the disciples.

The Gerasene demoniac

Mark 5, 1-20
Matt. 8, 28-34
Luke 8, 26-39

Christ has now crossed the Sea of Galilee into Gentile country. Matthew refers to it as the country of the Gadarenes - that is around Gadara - but the place is generally thought to have been near modern Khersa, near Magdala.

Violent lunatics, like lepers, were cast out of the towns and villages.

When Christ asks for the name of the evil spirit possessing the man, he replies, 'Legion'. A Roman legion numbered 6000 soldiers. He may have been identifying himself with all the spirits of the dead in the burial ground.

The transfer of the evil spirit into the pigs is quite unlike any-thing else Jesus is recorded to have done. Would he, in fact, deliberately destroy the pigs and the pig owner's property? He is not recorded as giving a definite order to that effect. Pigs, in Jewish eyes, were regarded as unclean animals, though it is doubtful whether Jesus would take that view of anything in God's creation. The disciples were possibly too frightened of the lunatic to be near enough to hear accurately what was said, and the swine-herds would have to blame someone for the loss of their animals which might well have stampeded at the noisy encounter.

The man is healed but Jesus forbids him to return to Galilee with them. Instead he is to broadcast the news of what has happened, to his own people. The fact that the man was a Gentile would account for Christ's attitude.

Jairus's daughter and the woman with the haemorrhage

Mark **5**, 21-43   Matthew's account of these two incidents is much briefer than the
Matt. **9**, 18-26   other writers'. Notice that everywhere Jesus goes at this time he is
Luke **8**, 40-56   beset by large crowds.

The president of a synagogue, in charge of its services, would be quite important and belong to the class of church rulers who were generally opposed to Christ, but his deep distress would override his hostility.

The woman who touched Jesus would be specially worried because her illness was considered by the Law of Moses to make her 'unclean' (Leviticus **15**, 25). Luke, as a doctor, omits the statements of the other writers that she had spent all her money on doctors, and, if anything, was worse as a consequence.

The commotion Jesus found round the death-bed was usual. It survived from an ancient belief that noise would frighten away evil spirits. By Rabbinic rule, the poorest people would be provided with two fluteplayers and one mourning woman. The synagogue president would have many more paid mourners.

The words, 'Talitha cum' given in Mark are the actual Aramaic words Jesus spoke. Notice Christ's practical mind: the child was being overwhelmed by fuss when after her illness she needed food.

Two other occasions when Jesus raised the dead were the incidents concerning the widow of Nain's son and Lazarus. It has been suggested that Jairus's daughter was not dead. Jesus indeed said that she was asleep - possibly in a coma. We do not know. It is unlikely that the people in the house would not recognise death, and death is referred to elsewhere by Jesus as a sleep (cf., John **11**, 11 - Lazarus).

Christ sends out the apostles

Mark **6**, 7-13   Take special note of Christ's directions to the apostles:
Matt. **9**, 35-38   To remain with only one house as their base during their mission
    10, 1, 5-15   in any locality was important. Eastern hospitality would expect
Luke **9**, 1-6, 10   a visitor to go from house to house, thus wasting much time.

To shake from their feet the dust of any place that rejected them. This was a general Jewish custom on leaving Gentile soil.

Anointing with oil was a common accompaniment to healing and was much used by the Jews.

Notice that the apostles were successful and returned later to report to Jesus.

33

The murder of John the Baptist

Mark **6**, 14-29
Matt. **14**, 1-12
Luke **9**, 7-9

This is the fourth and last episode in our study of John the Baptist. Here, Herod is clearly afraid because he has killed John and fears that Christ is his re-incarnation.

Herod (Antipas) had married Herodias, his half-brother's wife, having met her on a journey to Rome. He had persuaded her to leave her husband and to live with him, together with her grown-up daughter, Salome, who would be in her teens. His former wife, Aretas, daughter of an Arabian emir, did not wait for a divorce but fled back to her father, who in anger, assembled an army and inflicted a heavy defeat on Herod.

It seems likely that the whole situation on Herod's birthday was cunningly contrived by Herodias who hated John for denouncing her as Herod's mistress. It would be very unusual for a princess to perform like a dancing girl, but her mother obviously took advantage of what had become a drunken debauch and used her daughter to achieve her ambition.

Feeding of the five thousand and walking on the lake

Mark **6**, 30-56
Matt. **14**, 13-36
Luke **9**, 11-17
(John **6**, 1-21)

The miracle of the feeding of the five thousand is recorded in all four gospels. Attempts to explain it away by supposing that everyone present ate their own food are not satisfactory. It made a deep impression on the crowd, as a result of which, according to the Fourth Gospel, the men present wanted to carry Jesus away and proclaim him King. This, of course, was the reverse of what Jesus wanted, recalling one of his temptations in the wilderness, and he slipped away into the adjoining hills. He performed the miracle, as always, out of compassion.

Walking on the sea

Christ's walking on the sea is not recorded in Luke. Jesus, praying on the hillside, turns to observe his disciples having difficulty with their boat. (Anyone who has seen photographs taken by moonlight in Galilee will know how detail can be easily seen at a distance, almost as well as by day). He immediately goes to them. Matthew describes Peter's dramatic attempt to walk to Jesus.

Though this miracle may have taken place as described, one has to recognise that the Greek phrase here for walking *on* the lake could be equally well translated as walking *by* the lake, but this interpretation would create difficulties in the text.

Mark and Matthew emphasise Christ's enormous popularity when he reached the other side of the Sea of Galilee among the Gentiles in Genneseret.

34

The Pharisees and the tradition of washing

Mark 7, 1-23

Matt. 15, 1-20

The washing of hands mentioned here is ceremonial. It is not suggested that the disciples ate food with dirt on their hands.

When Jews returned from the market place or elsewhere, they washed ceremonially before they ate in order to avoid religious defilement through contact with Gentiles and with legally unclean objects. Pharisees washed up to their elbows. This custom stems from a very ancient belief in evil spirits inhabiting certain objects (cf., also the touching of a leper or a dead body).

Christ answers by saying that:

1. Religious impurity is not a physical matter at all but a mental and moral one. A man is not made impure by the food he eats, but by his thoughts. There are thirteen forms of evil listed here that proceed from evil thoughts.
2. Sometimes the Tradition of the Elders could even annul God's law as given in the Ten Commandments.

He cites the case of 'Corban'. If a man says 'Corban' over his property then it is consecrated to the Temple for the purpose of providing sacrifices ('Corban' means 'devoted to sacred use'). It could not then be used to help his parents, who might well be destitute, thus breaking the Law of God, 'Honour thy father and thy mother'.

The question of religious impurity was very important in the early church, as we see later in the New Testament. Jewish Christians at first found it very difficult to eat with Gentile Christians because of these traditions. The words of Christ here were very important to them.

The Syrophoenician woman

Mark 7, 24-30

Matt. 15, 21-28

Christ for a while leaves Galilee, because of the growing hostility of the Pharisees and possibly of Herod Antipas. No sooner does he find solitude just outside Galilee than this woman appears. Very few people ever had the ability to reply to Jesus. He was too clever for them, and too sincere. But this woman had a ready wit which delighted him and he healed her daughter. In any case he never refused anyone, Gentile or Jew.

In Palestine there were the wild dogs that roamed the streets and countryside and lived by scavenging. There were also the little dogs kept as pets. At table one placed all one's food, meat etc. on a piece of bread. After the meal, if you were poor, you ate the bread soaked with the juice of the meat you had eaten. But in many households it was thrown under the table for the little dogs to devour.

On what other occasion, do you remember, did Christ heal at a distance?

The healing of the deaf and 'dumb'

Mark **7**, 31-37   This miracle took place not very far from where the Geresene madman met Jesus. Jesus is still avoiding a return to Galilee, possibly because of the hostility of the authorities there.

Why did Jesus act in this way with the man who was deaf and had an impediment in his speech? It may have been that Jesus wanted to put the man at his ease since, being deaf, he would not know what was happening to him. He would recognise the use of saliva as an ancient method of healing.

The feeding of the four thousand

Mark **8**, 1-21   Jesus, having fed the five thousand, was likely to repeat this
Matt. **15**, 29-39   miracle on occasions when he met great crowds who were in need
16, 1-12   of food. Notice the difference between this miracle and the feeding of the five thousand:
1. It takes place among Gentiles, not Jews.
2. The people had been with Christ three days.
3. There were seven loaves, not five.
4. Four thousand people were fed.
5. The type of basket here, unlike that of the feeding of the five thousand, was similar to the rope basket by which St Paul escaped from Damascus.

Jesus here is as much concerned about the plight of Gentiles who had devotedly followed him, as he was previously about his own people.

Jesus distressed by both the Pharisees and his own disciples
Following on the miracle, note that Jesus is distressed by the unbelief of the Pharisees - and Sadducees (Matt. **16**, 1) - and the lack of understanding in his disciples.

Christ's claim to forgive sins, to be Lord of the Sabbath and to challenge the Oral Law so shocked the Pharisees that they felt that there should be a special sign, apart from the miracles, to prove the truth of what he said.

The disciples, on the other hand, though they have witnessed the miracles of feeding are worried because they are almost without bread. They misunderstand the leaven of the Pharisees by which Jesus meant their hypocrisy, and the leaven of Herod, meaning his worldliness. They take the word leaven literally and think they are not to buy it from the Pharisees or from Herod.

The blind man of Bethsaida

Mark **8**, 22-26	In Mark Jesus gives a gradual cure using the popular medium of
Matt. **9**, 27-34	spittle.

In Matthew we have two blind men, and the records may be connected, or slightly confused with each other. In addition, in Matthew Christ is recorded as healing a dumb man with a devil.

Six parables of the Kingdom

Mark **4**, 30-34	*The mustard seed; the leaven*
Matt. **13**, 31-35	These two parables show the power of the Kingdom of God to
Luke **13**, 18-21	grow from many small beginnings (cf., The Christian Church).

Matt. **13**, 24-30,	*The wheat and the weeds; the dragnet*
36-43, 47-52	These two parables teach that the final judgment of men will be made by Christ, and, unlike men during their lifetime, he will make it without error. Since God has granted men freedom of choice, evil and good both flourish in the world.

Matt. **13**, 44-46	*The treasure; the pearl*
	These two parables teach us that once a man recognises the value of the Kingdom of God he may be willing to sacrifice everything else for it. (e.g. The rich young ruler Mark **10**, 17-27, who was not prepared to do so.) 'The new and the old' (v. 52) may refer to Christ's teaching and the law of the Old Testament.

Questions for revision

1. Why do you think Jesus taught by parable? Give a detailed account of one of his longer parables and explain how it applies equally today as it did when he first told it.
2. Why did John the Baptist in prison send messengers to Jesus? What did they ask him and how did he reply to them? When they had left Jesus talked to the crowd concerning John. What did he say?
3. Describe an incident in which Jesus helps a Gentile and another in which he helps a social outcast. Which gospel emphasises Jesus's special concern for such people?
4. Give an account of Christ's healing of the paralytic and mention two other occasions when the Pharisees expressed their hostility to him for other reasons.

The Sermon on the Mount

The Sermon on the Mount

Matt. **5, 6, 7.**   It is possible that the author of Matthew took the teaching of Jesus on different occasions and put it into these three chapters. Luke certainly has much of it distributed in various parts of his gospel, as we shall see in the following references.

How it was compiled does not really matter. What is really important is the fact that ever since it was accepted in the first century as a little handbook of faith and morals for Christians, it has remained a standard by which men in Christian countries have judged their own conduct and the conduct of their rulers. Today, when many people seem to challenge all authority, it still offers a pattern for living that can save us from our greatest fears and suffering.

Notice how Christ repeatedly traces the origin of good and evil, not to our possessions, but to our thinking. Adultery, for example, springs from lust, dishonesty from covetousness, murder from anger. 'As a man thinketh in his heart, so is he.'

The Beatitudes
Matt. 5, 1-12
Luke 6, 20-26

The word 'Beatitude' comes from the Latin *beatitudo* meaning 'happiness'. Here we see that Jesus teaches that true happiness springs largely from our own thinking and attitude to life. The happy man is one who desires for himself and for society the qualities of meekness, peacefulness, purity of thought and the desire to discover and do what is right.

Certain points about the Beatitudes should be noted. We do not know what Christ meant by 'poor in spirit'. It may mean people who feel a lack of spiritual life in themselves and are sincerely seeking it. The word 'mourn' refers not only to those bereaved but to all who are in sorrow. Meekness is not the opposite of courage, but of arrogance and self-centredness. 'Righteousness' here should be compared with Jesus's reference to the righteousness of the Pharisees in Matthew v. 20 which consisted solely in keeping the Oral Law. Persecution of Christians had become common when these words of Christ were first written down.

The passage in Luke that seems to correspond to Matthew's beatitudes is really quite different. It offers comfort to the poor,

the hungry, the sad and the persecuted promising them a rich
reward in the next life. There follows a condemnation of the
rich and those well-thought of in this life. Their prosperity will
come to an end.

The Duty of Christians

Matt. **5**, 13-16
Mark **4**, 21-23
Luke **8**, 16-18
     11, 33

The Jewish nation had always prided itself upon being God's
chosen people. Jesus is saying that those who are listening to him
really must be so.

The sea of Galilee produced enormous quantities of fish, which
were exported to various parts of the Empire. This could only be
done by the use of salt as a preservative. Christians therefore must
preserve what is good in society and save it from corruption.

Artificial light was very precious in Christ's day. Christians must,
by their good deeds, be a light in a dark world. (cf., The great
assize, Matt. **25**, 31-46). A bushel was a container for measuring
meal. It would occasionally be turned upside down and used as a
stand.

Jesus and the Jewish Law

Matt. **5**, 17-48

The Jewish Law (the Torah) came from the first five books of the
Old Testament and its interpretation by the lawyers or scribes
(e.g. what exactly was 'work' on the Sabbath) was known as the
Oral Law, or the Traditions of the Elders.

Jesus showed great respect for the Torah. Notice his approval of
the rich young ruler for keeping the Ten Commandments. 'Do not
suppose,' he says, 'I have come to abolish the Law and the
Prophets; I did not come to abolish but to complete it' (or 'fulfil'
it). By this Jesus meant that he wished to bring out the full
meaning and purpose of the Law.

On the other hand, the Oral Law, as laid down by the Scribes,
consisted of 619 regulations, which were quite beyond the ability
of the common people to learn or understand. To Jesus this was a
tragic situation, so he largely ignored the Scribal regulations and
taking some of the principal laws from the Torah, we find him
here explaining their full meaning.

Matt. **5**, 21-26
Luke **12**, 58-59

The sixth commandment: You shall not kill
Jesus takes this commandment a stage back. What is the cause of
murder? Anger. Therefore anger is to be condemned. The
Synagogue Council, v. 22, was responsible for the moral order in
the community. 'The hell of fire' or the fires of hell', v. 22, refers

to the smouldering pit of Gehenna outside the walls of Jerusalem where the city's rubbish was dumped and where the bodies of criminals were thrown. In vv. 23-26 it is obvious that anger can destroy true worship and lead even to the pit of Gehenna. The whole passage teaches that Christ's followers should right wrongs and misunderstandings as early as possible.

Matt. **5**, 27-32
Luke **16**, 18

The seventh commandment: You shall not commit adultery
Again Jesus traces the cause: lustful thinking. Unchecked, it may lead to adultery. If we realise the misery adultery can bring to an otherwise happy family we see the force of 'if your right eye causes you to sin. . . .' Jesus permits divorce only on the grounds of unchastity (the exceptive clause). (cf., Luke **16**, 18 where divorce is condemned in all cases and there is no exceptive clause.) For the positive side of marriage cf., Mark **10**, 2-12.

Matt. **5**, 33-37
23, 16-22

The third commandment: You shall not swear falsely
The Jews in Christ's day used oaths sometimes blasphemously, taking the name of God in vain. But they also used oaths with the intention of deceiving. For example to swear 'by Jerusalem' to do something was invalid, said the Scribes, unless facing Jerusalem. Jesus says swear not at all - a Christian's word should be his bond.

Matt. **5**, 38-42
Luke **6**, 29-30

Retaliation: An eye for an eye
The Torah limited revenge. Amongst other nations in Moses' time revenge could be very terrible. Jesus forbids revenge. According to Jesus it shows far greater strength of character to refrain from retaliation. This is not as fantastic as it seems. Consider, for example, the motives behind our own penal system, to correct rather than to punish. Jesus won the respect of Pilate; the early Christians won that of both their judges and spectators by their returning of good for evil. The extra mile Jesus commands is better understood when we realise that in Palestine a Roman soldier could compel a Jew to carry his equipment for one Roman mile (1.48 km). cf., Simon of Cyrene (Mark **15**, 21).

Matt. **5**, 43-48
Luke **6**, 27, 28,
32-36

The law of love: Hate your enemy
This command cannot be found in the Torah. In practice, however, the Jews may have felt themselves justified in their hatred say of the Samaritans, because they looked upon them as enemies of God. 'Neighbour' to the Jews meant merely 'fellow Jews'. Gentiles were often referred to contemptuously as 'dogs' (unclean animals). The

word 'love' as used here is a Greek word meaning 'to have concern for the welfare of'. The Christian obligation is to pray for and to do good to his enemies. (cf., The good Samaritan.)

Matt. **6**, 1-18	*Beware of hypocrisy: almsgiving, prayer and fasting*
7, 7-11	In these Christian duties Jesus emphasises not the action but the
Luke **11**, 1-13	motive.

Almsgiving   This was not compulsory according to Jewish Law but was done to obtain special merit in the sight of God and clearly also in the sight of men! The Christian must be generous to those in need, (cf. Dives and Lazarus, Luke **16**, 19-31) but his giving must be done in secret. Compare also the story of the widow's mite, Mark **12**, 41-44.

Prayer   Jews, like Muslims, at the daily hour of prayer, if unable to join in public worship could say their prayers wherever they happened to be. Jesus realised the temptation to false piety this custom could develop, when people made a habit of being late for synagogue and saying their prayers in the street. Christians must not make a show of praying; they should pray thoughtfully and not rely on much meaningless repetition. The Lord's Prayer is notable for its brevity, simplicity, unselfishness and spirituality; only one material gift is asked for and that, the simplest. Luke **11**, 1-13 gives a shortened form of the Lord's Prayer but also adds the parable of the importunate neighbour, who persists in knocking his friend up in the middle of the night for bread. God, on the other hand, is only too eager to answer prayer. 'Ask and it shall be given you, seek and you shall find, knock and it will be opened to you'.

Fasting   Here again Christians should fast secretly, not like the hypocrites who smeared their faces with ash to draw attention to their sufferings.

Some rules for the guidance of Christians

Matt. **6**, 19-24	
Luke **11**, 34-36	*Money*
12, 33-34	Good works (treasure in heaven) must be more important than
16, 13	money and property, for the former last into eternity while the

latter cause worry and anxiety and can easily disappear, and in any case are useless in the next world. (cf., The parable of the rich fool - Luke **12**, 13-21.)

Jesus also makes a comparison between the physical eye which lights the body and the inner light, (cf., conscience), which lights the mind.

Matt. **6**, 25-34	*Worry*
Luke **12**, 22-32	

Jesus here is not criticising proper forethought and planning for the future, but the worry and anxiety that people allow themselves to suffer in regard to it. This is due to lack of faith in God. The Christian should do all he can about the future, but things he cannot do and the problems he cannot solve he should leave with confidence in the hands of God. Again he emphasises that material things should be secondary in the life of a Christian. Foremost should be his desire to do God's will.

The lilies referred to were the anemones that grow in profusion in Galilee. The grass in the fields was dried and used as fuel.

Matt. **7**, 1-6	*Judging other people*
Luke **6**, 37-42	
Mark **4**, 24	

Jesus insists that Christians should be charitable and generous in their judgment of other people. Most of us have sins as bad as, if not worse than, those whom we criticise. (In any case, a man who is continually criticising other people is by doing so revealing his own lack of confidence.)

Yet the disciples must discriminate between those who will listen to the gospel and those who will not. Christ had many unpleasant experiences of Pharisees who treated his teaching with contempt. It was as useless to offer them the truth as it was to try to feed swine with pearls. Note his direction to the seventy he sent out (Mark **6**, 11).

Matt. **7**, 7-11	*Prayer*

All sincere prayer is answered. Jesus makes a comparison between an earthly father and God. In Luke, Jesus is recorded as saying that God will give the Holy Spirit to those who ask him; in Matthew, 'the Holy Spirit' is replaced by the phrase 'good things'.

Matt. **7**, 12	*The golden rule*
Luke **6**, 31	

Both the Jews and other religious teachers, like Confucius, state the negative side of this rule - do not do to others what you would not wish them to do to you. Christ's positive command, on the contrary, demands action.

The only way
Matt. **7**, 13-29
Luke **13**, 22-30
Luke **6**, 43-49

The rest of the sermon is devoted to showing that there is only one way to salvation. Christ is offering men the way of life for which God really made them. The majority of men, he warns them, will not take it, because their alternative way of life is easier and seems more attractive.

He warns them against two dangers that soon appeared after he left them: false teachers who took money and hospitality from credulous listeners, and sorcerers and necromancers (people who supposedly worked magic by communication with the dead) who used Christ's name among others when performing strange rites and casting spells. Finally, in the story of the two houses, he insists that his followers will be saved not simply by their faith but by their actions.

Questions for revision

1. What was Christ's attitude to the Law? By considering three of the Ten Commandments show how he gave the Mosaic law a fuller meaning.
2. What religious practices did Jesus suggest should be carried out secretly? In each case what kind of behaviour did Jesus condemn and why did he condemn it?
3. What did Jesus teach in the Sermon on the Mount about a. prayer; b. trust in God; c. the duty of Christians? Mention any occasions you can think of where Jesus put this teaching into practice in his own life.

Christ's Work of Teaching and Healing continued

Christ rejected by the Samaritans

Luke **9**, 51-56   Note the hostility of the Samaritans. They had their own temple
on Mt Gerizim. Why should anyone, therefore, need to go to
Jerusalem, as Jesus was doing, for the Passover? James and John
were clearly very angry with the Samaritans. Their suggested
revenge may have earned for them the name Sons of Thunder, by
which they were known. Jesus teaches them a lesson in tolerance.
The words 'received up' probably refer to his ascension.

The three would-be followers

Luke **9**, 57-62   Jesus stresses the urgency, and the severity of the work these men
Matt. **8**, 19-22   hoped to do. (In Matthew there are only two, one of whom is a
scribe.) If they are to follow Christ, they must make a complete
break with their old way of life. 'Leave the dead. . . .' may mean
leave those who are spiritually dead to bury their dead.

The mission of the Seventy

Luke **10**, 1-24   This event must not be confused with the sending out of the
Matt. **11**, 20-30 twelve apostles (p. 33) though Christ's directions to them are
similar. Seventy or seventy-two was considered to be the number
of nations in the world. While the sending out of the apostles
would be symbolic of sending the gospel to the Jews, the mission
of the Seventy would represent the larger field of Jew and Gentile
throughout the world - of special interest to Luke. Matthew
characteristically omits the event.

Christ is leaving Galilee and beginning his journey through
Perea to Jerusalem.

Note the directions given to the Seventy:
1. To go two by two.
2. To carry neither purse, scrip (wallet), nor shoes.
3. To waste no time on oriental courtesies on the way. Christ
   emphasises the urgency of their work.
4. To begin their mission with prayers for peace.
5. To eat and drink what is given to them.
6. Not to accept entertainment in many households.
7. To heal the sick and proclaim the Kingdom.
8. To shake off the dust of the cities that reject them.

Christ's prophecy (also in Matt. 11, 20-24) about the towns around the Sea of Galilee came true. Thirty years later their ruin when the Romans sacked them was so terrible that even the enemies of the Jews were sorry for them.

The return of the seventy

The Seventy returned with joy because of their success. Christ was greatly encouraged because this was the second occasion on which he had imparted to his followers his faith and power. This guaranteed that his work would be carried on when he left them.

Christ then prophesies the overthrow of evil - 'Satan falling from heaven' - wherever his work is done. To tread on snakes (serpents) and scorpions was a current metaphor for the victory of good over evil. But the fact that the disciples were in the Kingdom of God was more important than their power even to work miracles. To enter that kingdom one needed the simple, unquestioning faith of a little child, a condition not easy for 'the wise and the understanding' to accept. Matthew adds Christ's appeal to those 'who labour and are heavy laden' (Matt. 11, 28-30).

The good Samaritan
Luke 10, 25-37

The Jews were an exclusive race. The word 'neighbour' to them meant a fellow-Jew. This was quite unacceptable to Jesus and deliberately he makes a Samaritan the hero of his story. Notice, therefore, the question to which the parable is the answer. The lawyer may well be quoting Jesus in his statement about the two greatest commandments. They are taken from Deuteronomy 6, 4, 5 and Leviticus 19, 18. In this Old Testament setting 'neighbour' would certainly mean fellow-Jew.

The road from Jerusalem (610 metres) to Jericho (305 metres below sea-level) was a distance of thirty-four kilometres and known as the Bloody Way because it was infested with murdering robbers. Herod the Great had done much to make the road safe, but in Christ's time it was again very bad indeed.

The priest and Levite may have been afraid of ceremonial defilement in touching a dead body, but as they were on their way back from Jerusalem, it is more likely that they were simply scared of lurking robber bands. The Levites acted as assistants to the priests, fetching and carrying for them in preparing the sacrifices.

The Samaritan gave the equivalent of two days' wages for a working man to the innkeeper.

Notice that the lawyer, at the end of the story, could not bring himself even to pronounce the word 'Samaritan'.

Martha and Mary the sisters of Bethany

Luke 10, 38-42   The Fourth Gospel tells us that Martha and Mary lived with their brother, Lazarus, in Bethany, a village quite near Jerusalem. As at this time Jesus was nowhere near Jerusalem, the incident is misplaced, perhaps intentionally to be complementary to the Good Samaritan, teaching that love of one's neighbour must go hand in hand with making time to show our love for God by listening to him.

Martha's fault is not her activity but the fret and fuss behind it. Perhaps Jesus thought also that the meal was too elaborate, one simple course only being necessary.

Christ condemns the Pharisees and the lawyers

Luke 11, 37-54   In Luke this denunciation of the Scribes and Pharisees arises over
20, 45-47   Christ's refusal to wash ceremonially before a meal. Compare with
Matt. 23, 1-36   this the trouble that arose over the disciples' failure to do the same
Mark 12, 38-40   thing - Mark 7, 1-23 (p. 35). Christ condemned the Pharisees here because:
1. They were ceremonially clean, but impure in mind and motive.
2. They kept the Oral Law to the final syllable, even to the absurdity of giving a tenth of a few seeds or a stalk to God, but they had none of God's love in their hearts.
3. They liked prominence and the reverence of men (cf. their attitude to the chief seats in the synagogue, to alms-giving, fasting and praying in public.)

Then one of the lawyers (Scribes) argued with him. He just could not believe that Christ included Scribes in his denunciation. They considered themselves more distinguished than the Pharisees. They were the interpreters of the Law; Pharisees quoted them. But Christ criticises them also:
1. They crushed men with the burden of the Oral Law.
2. They rejected the prophets e.g. John the Baptist.
3. They kept the knowledge of God away from the people by declaring that they alone could interpret God's laws.

The reference in v. 51 'from Abel to Zechariah' means throughout all the recorded history of the Jews. Zechariah, the son of the High Priest was murdered in the Temple in 772 B.C. for prophesying that God would forsake the nation. Some people attributed the capture of Jerusalem by Nebuchadrezzar to divine vengence for this murder. In Matthew we have the same denunciation with one or two additions. In v. 8-12 Christ condemns the practice of giving titles to religious leaders. It can hardly be taken literally but it is a warning against pride as shown by the Pharisees, and a plea for brotherhood among Christ's followers. Verses 16-22 give additional evidence of the stupid and sometimes deceitful use of oaths.

The consequences of Christ's ministry

Luke 12, 1-12, 49-59
Matt. 10, 16-42

Christ gives here a very solemn warning to those who would be his followers. Pretence and hypocrisy, such as seen in the Pharisees will one day be exposed. His followers will be sincere. They will not fear anyone on earth who can deprive them of their bodily life, but only the devil who can destroy their souls. God's care for a single sparrow should remind them of God's great concern for them, especially when they suffer arrest and ill-treatment.

Christ's message will set fire to mankind and cause dissension and hatred, even between members of the same family.

In Matthew Christ adds further warnings: that his followers must expect to be hated by everyone, they will be sheep amongst wolves and be dragged before councils and rulers and flogged in the synagogues.

The duty of watchfulness

Luke 12, 35-48
Matt. 24, 45-51

Like men-servants waiting and preparing for the bridegroom at the marriage and the servant in charge of the household in his master's absence, Christ's followers should be conscientious and continually on the watch for they do not know when they will be called upon to give an account of what they have done.

The parable of the rich fool

Luke 12, 13-21

This parable was prompted by the behaviour of a man who in his greed wanted to use Jesus for his own ends. The laws of inheritance were clearly and fairly laid down for the Jews and obviously Jesus was not the one to whom this man should appeal. We can almost see him, however, elbowing his way to the front of the crowd and interrupting Christ's teaching. 'Beware of covetousness', says Jesus and proceeds with the parable about a man who thought only of his riches and how best he could enjoy them. It is the man's attitude, not his riches, that is condemned.

The need for repentance

Luke **13**, 1-9   Jesus here teaches an important lesson that has never been properly understood by all his followers: that whilst a man may bring calamities upon himself as a result of sin, God never intervenes to inflict calamities upon people because of their sins. Nevertheless, the parable of the fruitless fig tree warns us that there is a final judgement.

The Galileans referred to were probably Passover pilgrims who had provoked the Romans and had been massacred. These incidents happened frequently - 3000 on one occasion, 20 000 on another. Josephus, the Jewish historian, does not mention this incident.

The men in connection with the tower of Siloam were building an aqueduct to bring water into Jerusalem. (Pilate confiscated Corban to pay for their work.)

The object of the questioners may have been to arouse Christ's anger against the Romans and so get him into trouble with them.

A woman healed on the Sabbath

Luke **13**, 10-17   The woman is evidently suffering from curvature of the spine. The ruler of the synagogue attacks the people, rather than Jesus, but Jesus answers him with the clever analogy of the loosened ox or ass compared with the loosened woman. 'A daughter of Abraham' signified a Jewess.

A message to Herod Antipas

Luke **13**, 31-35   This may have been a desire of the Pharisees to get Jesus to
Matt. **23**, 37-39   Jerusalem and into the hands of the Sanhedrin, or it might well have been a friendly warning. Joanna, the wife of Chuza, Herod's steward, was one of the women who cared for Jesus.

We have also in both gospels Christ's prophecy about Jerusalem which refused to accept him.

The man with dropsy

Luke **14**, 1-6   The invitation to the Pharisees's house looks like an attempt to get evidence against him. Pharisees' motives were not usually friendly. Again Jesus maintains that human need is more important than Sabbath laws.

Humility

Luke **14**, 7-14   Real charity is giving something to someone from whom you would not expect any repayment.

The cost of discipleship

Luke 14, 25-35   Christ often stated his teaching in an extreme form so that people would not forget his words. The claims Christ makes upon anyone whose family is opposed to them may lead to great bitterness and even persecution. (This does happen in some parts of the world today when a Christian is a convert from another religion.) But the disciple must be prepared·if necessary to renounce all ties with those whom he loves.

The two short illustrations that follow teach us that we should weigh up the cost of discipleship before making a decision.

Christ's interest in the outcast
Luke 15

The lost sheep; The lost coin; The lost son
These three parables are told in reply to the Pharisees' criticism of the disreputable company Christ keeps - people whom they treat with contempt.

The ninety-nine 'righteous' persons Jesus speaks of is a sarcastic reference to the Pharisees who consider themselves above criticism. The ten silver coins were probably worn as an ornament round the forehead.

The younger son in the parable of the prodigal son would receive a third share of his father's property. He reached the depths of degradation when he became a swineherd because the Jews looked upon pigs as unclean animals.

The ring and the shoes given him on his return would indicate that from being a slave he would now be restored to sonship.

The elder son in some ways represents the hard and self-satisfied Pharisees who continually objected to Christ's love for sinners.

Parable of the unjust steward

Luke 16, 1-9   A steward (or bailiff) having mismanaged his employer's property is about to be dismissed by his master. He makes friends with the tenants at his master's expense. His master, when he hears of it, praises his servant for his cleverness (not for his dishonesty!)

The parable may teach that Christians should show in working for Christ some of the resourcefulness and shrewdness that worldly people reveal in their pursuit of the 'unrighteous mammon' (money).

Other explanations of this parable have been suggested but none is entirely satisfactory.

The right use of money
Luke 16, 10-17   In money matters Christians should be beyond reproach. If we are untrustworthy with the wealth of this world which God only lends us, he is not likely to entrust us with much in the next life. Jesus makes a sharp distinction between lives dominated by the worship of God and those dominated by the worship of money. The Pharisees scoff at him for this.

Verses 16-17 do not appear related to this passage. Jesus is again saying that John the Baptist marked the end of the old way of life and that the Gospel begins a new one. Note Christ's respect for the Law.

The parable of the rich man and Lazarus
Luke 16, 19-31   The rich man in this parable is often referred to as Dives (a. Latin word meaning 'rich').

Jesus is always guarded in his references to the afterlife. He leaves no doubt that there is one and that its nature will depend upon our faith and conduct in this one. Apart from this he usually refers to it in symbolic language known to his hearers. In this parable words such as 'Abraham's bosom', 'the great gulf', and the tormenting 'fire' are not to be taken literally. They are symbols like 'bridegroom' and 'heavenly banquet' used elsewhere to convey the idea of happiness in a future state.

Dives suffers not simply because he was rich but because of his selfish indifference to the needs of others, not even offering to Lazarus the food that he did not want himself.

This parable is a suitable reply to the Pharisees who were lovers of money and who scoffed at his teaching about it (v. 14). Jesus constantly refers to their selfish indifference towards those who needed their help.

A number of sayings and the parable of the master and servant
Luke 17, 1-10   'These little ones' in v. 2 refers, not to children, but to those who are weak and easily led.

The sycamine tree in v. 6 is probably a fig tree. Christ seems always amazed at the disciples' lack of faith.

The parable of the master and servant emphasises that the Kingdom of God is a gift to be asked for. It is not earned, since whatever we do we are still unworthy of it.

Healing of ten lepers
Luke 17, 11-19   Only the living death of leprosy could have brought the nine Jews in this incident into the company of a Samaritan. Note that the

50

lepers kept their distance. They would have to go to their priest to get a certificate of health in order to be re-admitted to their town or village. Luke would especially like this incident as he was writing his gospel for the Gentiles.

Apocalyptic sayings
Luke 17, 20-37

Apocalypse means a prophetic revelation, especially a vision in regard to the end of an era or the end of the world.

To the Pharisees' question as to when the Kingdom of God would come, he replied, 'It is in your midst' or 'within you' (the Greek text can mean either). He is saying, in fact, that the Kingdom began with him and is in the hearts and minds of those who accept him.

The rest of the passage describes the last days of humanity. Jesus says neither when nor how this will happen, but it will be unmistakeable. It seems that those who are taken will be saved; those who are left, doomed. Thus the reference to vultures in v. 37.

It is not always clear in the gospels when Jesus's words refer to the end of humanity and when he is referring to the destruction of Jerusalem and the Jewish state (A.D. 70). Sayings such as these, therefore, must be read cautiously with this problem in mind.

Parable of the unjust judge
Luke 18, 1-8

This parable teaches that though the Second Coming is delayed God will eventually see that justice is done. We should not lose hope but continue to pray, and be prepared. (cf., the importunate neighbour, Luke 11, 5-8).

Parable of the Pharisee and the publican
Luke 18, 9-14

The parable teaches the duty of humility in prayer. The Pharisee talked to God as if he were addressing an inferior. He was very proud that he went beyond the Law's requirements. Fasting was required only once a year, on the Day of Atonement; tithing was restricted to corn, wine, oil and cattle.

Zaccheus, the Publican
Luke 19, 1-10

Zaccheus would be an important official in Jericho. The sycamore-fig (not an English sycamore) which he climbed would be comparatively small with horizontal branches. We can imagine some of the crowd laughing at this man, whom they disliked, perched in the tree.

Jesus would possibly lose friends, because they would not consider it respectable for him to go to this man's house and be in the company of the sort of friends he had. Notice Christ's effect upon him.

Compare this man with Levi (Mark **2**, 13-17).

Questions for revision

1. In two famous parables, the good Samaritan and the prodigal son, Jesus uses altogether six main characters. By reference to each of these characters and how Jesus uses them show the lessons he was teaching to his hearers.
2. Describe the mission of the Seventy - Christ's instructions to them, their report on their work when they returned and what comments Jesus made.
3. Say what you have gathered about Christ's teaching on the use of money. Describe one parable, and if you can recall it, one incident in the gospels which re-inforces his teaching.
4. Outline the six criticisms Jesus made of the scribes and Pharisees on the occasion when he failed to wash ceremonially before a meal. How would they have to change their lives to conform with Christ's commandment 'Thou shalt love thy neighbour as thyself'?

Caesarea Philippi and the Road to Death

Caesarea Philippi and Peter's confession

Mark **8**, 27-30   Christ's work in Galilee is almost finished and he is about to begin
Matt. **16**, 13-20   his final journey to Jerusalem.
Luke **9**, 18-21   In the Synoptic Gospels we find that Jesus does not reveal
himself as Messiah, since this could well have been a signal for
revolt, especially in Galilee where rebellion against Rome was
most likely to break out (see Introduction - Palestine). That he
was very careful about this is evident from the fact that when he
enquired who people thought he was the name Messiah was never
mentioned. But the time has now come when his disciples must
know.

He takes them thirty-four kilometres north of the Sea of
Galilee to Caesarea Philippi for quiet instruction. There we have a
very important conversation between Christ and Peter. It is
interesting to compare the records in the three gospels. Matthew's
is the most detailed.

The word 'Christos' (Christ) is the equivalent in Greek of the
word 'Messiah' and Peter has had the remarkable perception to see
that Jesus is Messiah, though in character he is totally unlike the
current ideas of a Jewish deliverer.

Peter and the Church
In Aramaic the word for 'Peter' and for 'rock' is 'cepha' (Paul
refers to him as 'Cephas'). In Greek 'Peter' is 'Petros' and 'rock' is
'petra'. Thus when Jesus says that upon 'this rock' he will build his
church, there is little doubt that he is singling out Peter as the head
of the Church. It is believed that later Peter became the head of
the Church in Rome and is buried beneath St Peter's.

Jesus also gives Peter (and later, the other disciples, Matt. **18**,
18-20) the power to forbid (bind) and to allow (loose) - that is the
authority to govern the way of life within the Church.

Christ still demands secrecy - until, at least, he arrives in
Jerusalem. Once there, by his actions and words, he indicates
clearly who he is.

Christ foretells his suffering and that of his followers

Mark **8**, 31 -
Mark **9**, 1
Matt. **16**, 21-28
Luke **9**, 22-27

The words of Christ in this passage must have come as a terrible shock to his followers. At Caesarea Philippi he had admitted to them that he was Messiah. However different Christ was from current expectations, the disciples would now expect that his ministry would at least end in triumph, with a glorious new era of freedom and prosperity for the Jewish nation. Imagine, then, the effect of these words forecasting his own horrible death and the persecution that also awaited them. His disciples never understood these prophecies nor accepted them till the actual events took place.

In Matthew and Mark we are told that Peter, finding Christ's words unbelievable, argues with him. Christ, having made his decision to go to Jerusalem and die, finds Peter's criticism like the voice of Satan tempting him, perhaps, to take an easier way out.

'Whoever would save his life' means the man who thinks only of self and self-preservation, as the opposite of the man 'who would lose his life', that is, forget himself in the service of Christ.

At the conclusion of his words to them Jesus says that many of his followers would live to see Christ's Kingdom come with power. This was taken to mean that they would see Christ return to earth - the Second Coming. But Jesus himself declared that he did not know when that would be. But the Kingdom did, in fact, come with power, among the disciples at Pentecost (Acts **2**), and territorially it spread with great rapidity, reaching Rome - the Emperor's own household - before many of them died.

The Transfiguration

Mark **9**, 2-13
Matt. **17**, 1-13
Luke **9**, 28-36

A very important experience for Peter, James and John. They were beset by conflicting fears and hopes. A Messiah who was to die wretchedly in the hands of his enemies seemed impossible. Then suddenly on this mountain they shared a wonderful vision of Christ in radiant glory with Moses, the great lawgiver, and Elijah the greatest of all the prophets. The presence of Moses and Elijah symbolised that Christ unites and finally fulfils all the Law and the prophecy of Jewish history. This vision would confirm Peter's belief in Jesus as Messiah.

Wishing to prolong the fading vision, he suggests that they should build three shelters but there comes a voice from heaven (Jesus had already heard God's voice at his baptism) declaring Jesus to be God's son.

The brilliant cloud was known in Jewish history as the

Shekinah. It led the Israelites out of Egypt; it was seen over Mount Sinai when Moses went up to meet God; it again appears at Christ's Ascension.

The Jews have always felt that Elijah would return to earth as the forerunner of Messiah and his Kingdom. Jesus assured the disciples that he had already returned in the person of John the Baptist.

The epileptic boy
Mark 9, 14-32
Matt. 17. 24-27
Luke 9, 37-45

The amazement the crowd showed, mentioned in Mark, at seeing Christ, may have been due to a certain radiance about his features that remained after the Transfiguration. Often, after this, he seems to have inspired awe in people.

Again he is astonished at people's lack of faith. It almost reduces him to despair, especially in face of the disciples' failure here, when earlier, after he had sent them out to preach and heal, they had returned jubilant with success.

As they continue their journey through Galilee Jesus again reminds them of the horrible fate that awaits him in Jerusalem. It seems that the disciples, with their minds full of the Transfiguration and Christ's wonderful power over evil, cannot comprehend how such things can happen to him.

The tribute money
Matt. 17, 24-27

All Jews paid Temple tribute (see Introduction - Palestine). There seems a light-hearted note in what Christ said. As Son of God he should not pay tribute! If we are to take the words that follow literally, we have here the only occasion on which Jesus performed a miracle for his own benefit. This temptation was faced and dismissed at the beginning of his ministry when as a starving man, he was tempted to turn stones into bread. It would be more consistent for us to think that Jesus is again using symbolism and is saying to Peter, in effect, that the price of a fish was all that was necessary to raise the tax payment.

Conversation with the disciples
Mark 9, 33-50
Matt. 18, 1-35
Luke 9, 46-50

Still the disciples prefer to ignore Christ's prophecy about his death and prefer to argue as to which of them would be greatest in his Kingdom. (Note the same argument on the way to the Last Supper, and also James' and John's request.)

Christ counters their selfish ambitions by informing them that to enter the Kingdom they must have the virtues of a little child, that is humility and simple faith. They must also seek the lost and be careful not to discourage new converts.

The millstone was of the type pulled round by a donkey. To be drowned in such a manner was both a Greek and a Roman punishment for killing one's father.

The words used by Christ here about general temptation are used by him in connection with adultery in the Sermon on the Mount.

Forgiveness

Jesus lays down four steps for a Christian to take if anyone has committed a serious wrong against him:
1. Talk to him privately.
2. Talk to him before two witnesses.
3. Take the matter to the Church.
4. Finally he would have to take the offender to the Courts.

'As a Gentile and a tax collector' refers rather to the way the average Jew looked upon such people.

The rabbis taught that a man should forgive his enemies three times; Jesus taught that forgiveness should be unlimited.

The parable of the unmerciful servant in Matthew emphasises that our sins are forgiven only if we forgive those who sin against us.

Marriage and divorce

Mark **10**, 1-12

Matt. **5**, 27, 28, 31, 32

Matt. **19**, 1-12

Luke **16**, 18

The status of women in the ancient world varied.

Under Roman law husband and wife were on terms of equality, and either could divorce the other on the flimsiest pretext. All that was required was the presence of seven witnesses to hear the statement of divorce. Women, except slave women who had been freed to marry, could recover their dowry and marry again.

Under Jewish law, however, the woman could not legally divorce her husband, though in certain circumstances she could compel her husband to divorce her. According to Deuteronomy **24**, 1-4 she could remarry. This would be necessary for most women, as they would require a man's financial support.

In what circumstances could a man divorce his wife? According to the Law, a husband *must* divorce his wife, if she was not a virgin when he married her (assuming she was not a widow). Apart from this, he has the right to divorce her 'if she finds no favour in his eyes because he has found some indecency in her' (Deuteronomy **24**, 1-4).

The question for the rabbis was always what 'indecency' was.

Rabbi Shamai taught that it could be no less than adultery; Rabbi Hillel, that it could be a merely trivial matter such as her inability to cook properly.

Christ's teaching
We should expect Christ's standards to be higher as, indeed, they were. The Mosaic Law, he points out, was given because the people were then primitive in understanding as a result of slavery, and they had been much influenced by pagan practices. Now it was different. There was to be no divorce at all. Marriage from the beginning of creation was intended to be permanent. 'Those whom God has joined together, let no man put asunder.'

On the other hand, in Matthew 5, 32, and 19, 9, we have the *exceptive clause*. Jesus allows divorce in the case where a man finds the woman unchaste. The Greek word used here means fornication before marriage or adultery after marriage. He can remarry - because the marriage is annulled - but she cannot.

So what is Christ's teaching - no divorce at all or divorce in the case of unchastity? No one can be certain. But on the positive side it is clear that Christ teaches that marriage is a sacred and solemn contract made in the sight of God, not to be broken for trivial or selfish reasons.

Many Christians believe that the words of Christ here cannot be taken as a present day legal ruling and that in this complex world, Christ would demand simply that in normal circumstances marriage should be regarded as indissoluble. But in abnormal circumstances (e.g. incurable insanity, chronic infidelity) whatever is done should be governed by love and consideration for the other partner and the children of the marriage.

Christ blesses the children

Mark **10**, 13-16   It is interesting to note that in Mark and Matthew this incident
Matt. **19**, 13-15   occurs after Christ has given his teaching about Christian marriage.
Luke **18**, 15-17   He has made it clear that marriage should be a solemn and binding contract which should provide for the children of the marriage a happy and secure home.

It was usual for mothers to take their children to the president of their synagogue for his blessing, and they evidently sought Christ's blessing too since he upheld the sacredness of marriage.

His interest in and concern for children is shown on a number of occasions. He is indignant here that his disciples should try to

turn them away and he often referred to their humility and trust
as the ideal qualities for entry into God's Kingdom.

The rich young ruler

Mark **10**, 17-31   The twelve disciples had given up all their worldly possessions to
Matt. **19**, 16-30   follow Christ. But it is clear that his teaching for those outside
Luke **18**, 18-30   this special group is stewardship. One day, we shall be required to
give an account of how we have used whatever we have had in this
life - whether ten talents or one.

      Why then had this young man to get rid of all his possessions?
It was possibly a case of worshipping God or money. Christ probably recognised that the young ruler was incapable of acting as
steward of his possessions. Money had become his god, and the
only solution was to get rid of it. Christ suggests that this is often
the case. With the accumulation of money, there can come a
change for the worse in character; thus it is difficult for those who
have riches to enter the Kingdom of God.

      The disciples were astonished, because in those days wealth was
commonly considered as a sign of God's favour, but Jesus says
that only by the grace of God can a rich man avoid the dangers
and temptations of riches and fulfil the obligations of the
Kingdom.

      Those who have given up everything for him will, even in this
life, receive ample compensation in the brotherhood of the
Kingdom.

      'Why do you call me "good"? No one is good but God.' There
is no evidence that Christ was anything but absolute goodness - no
record or confession of sin. It may be that Christ wanted the
young man to think carefully about his words. In Christ's day it
was a customary and unthinking introduction to say, 'Good
rabbi' when approaching a teacher. Christ disliked flattery or
insincerity. Matthew modifies these words, obviously thinking
them out of place here.

The labourers in the vineyard

Matt. **20**, 1-16   The parable teaches God's generosity. The men who came late
into the vineyard to work probably represent tax-collectors,
prostitutes and others whose lives up to then had no merit at all
in the eyes of God. Like the parables of the unprofitable servant
(Luke **17**, 7-10) and the prodigal son (Luke **15**, 11-32) it suggests
that the Kingdom of God is not really earned - it is God's gift to
those who truly seek it.

Christ takes a decisive step

Mark **10**, 32-34   The amazement and fear expressed in Mark at Jesus taking the
Matt. **20**, 17-19   road south to Jerusalem suggests that the disciples were beginning
Luke **18**, 31-34   to realise the dangers the capital held for their master.

The ambitions of James and John

Mark **10**, 35-45   Jesus had just spoken for the third time in recent days of his
Matt. **20**, 20-28   coming death. After the first Peter had rebuked him; after the
second, the disciples had argued as to who would be greatest in
the Kingdom; after the third time James and John (in Matthew,
their mother) asked for special privileges in the Kingdom. The
'cup' is the cup of suffering; the 'baptism' is the agony of death.
Both men suffered, in fact, for Christ. Their mother was probably
Salome, Mary's sister, and they would therefore think that they
were entitled to special privileges.

Blind Bartimaeus   The cry of Bartimaeus is interesting because he addresses Christ as
Mark **10**, 46-52   The Son of David'. Now Messiah was to come 'of the house of
Matt. **20**, 29-34   David' and this meant that the beggar was addressing Jesus as
Luke **18**, 35-43   Messiah. Christ is not therefore bothering any more to conceal
that he is Messiah. He does not rebuke Bartimaeus. Notice that in
Matthew there are two men - one possibly Bartimaeus.

Questions for revision

1. Relate in detail what happened at Caesarea Philippi. Why was
   this conversation necessary before Christ's final visit to
   Jerusalem? What did Christ go on to say about his own future
   and why was this incomprehensible to the disciples?
2. Describe the Transfiguration. Why was this experience very
   important to Christ's disciples?
3. What were the current views in Christ's day about marriage
   and divorce? Outline Christ's teaching and say what you think
   should be the Christian attitude today.

c   59

Holy Week

Jesus no longer hides the fact that he is Messiah, but shows it as much by what he does as by what he says. His ride into Jerusalem, the demonstration he allows, his action in the Temple and his parables all stress that he looks upon himself as Messiah and the Son of God.

The Triumphal entry

Mark **11**, 1-11
Matt. **21**, 1-11
Luke **19**, 28-44

Notice the minute details that Jesus gives about the donkey (and, in Matthew, her foal). Jesus seems to be making a number of arrangement for this important week before his death (cf., the Last Supper). The donkey evidently belonged to a friend. A horse was a symbol of war; an ass, a symbol of peace. Jesus no doubt had in mind the prophecy of Zechariah **9**, 9 about Messiah 'Rejoice, daughter of Zion. . . . for see, your king is coming to you, his cause won, his victory gained, humble and mounted on an ass, on a foal, the young of a she ass'.

'Blessings on him who comes in the name of the Lord' - a customary greeting given to pilgrims arriving for the Passover. It would be reasonable to believe that some of the crowd recognised Jesus as Messiah, but all accepted him as a great prophet.

His lament over Jerusalem, given in Luke, is truly prophetic. In A.D. 70 Titus, the Roman general, destroyed Jerusalem. The massacre was so horrible that even the Jews' enemies were sorry for them.

The cursing of the fig tree

Mark **11**, 12-14
       20-26
Matt. **21**, 18-22

This incident is best considered as an acted parable and prophecy about the Jewish nation. Professing to be God's people without doing his will would bring disaster. The incident also demonstrates the miraculous power of faith.

The cleansing of the Temple

Mark **11**, 15-19
Matt. **21**, 12-17
Luke **19**, 45-48

A market for the sale of animals specially selected for sacrifice, and for the changing of money had been set up in the Gentiles' Court during the Passover. The Jews were required to pay the Temple tax in Temple coinage, as money from various parts of the Empire might well have the heads of pagan gods and other idolatrous symbols on them. The traders made an excessive profit especially out of visitors to the capital. This is clear from Christ's outburst, 'Scripture says, "My house shall be called a house of prayer", but you are making it a robbers' cave!' (Matthew). Having driven out the traders and thrown over their stalls he then angrily forbade anyone to use the Gentiles' court as a thoroughfare.

All this Jesus did in open defiance of the High Priest and the priesthood who derived a large income from the Temple trading. But his bold action together with his miracles of healing made him so popular that they were quite powerless to restrain him. They turned to the only weapon possible at this point - debate. By asking him questions they were convinced that they could get this peasant leader into trouble somehow or make him look foolish in the eyes of the people.

The authorities challenge Christ

Mark **11**, 27-33
Luke **20**, 1-8
Matt. **21**, 23-27

On the following day therefore Jesus is challenged by what seems to be an official deputation. What authority, they ask, has he for policing the Temple, scattering the money changers and closing the Gentile court as a thoroughfare? Christ's reply is not a clever evasion. It was born of his anger against the Pharisees for their treatment of John the Baptist, and their resulting cowardice. They refused to recognise John but they had not the courage to deny his authority in front of the people who accepted him as a great prophet.

The question of taxes

Mark **12**, 13-17
Matt. **22**, 15-22
Luke **20**, 20-26

This matter concerned the Roman occupation. The Pharisees were opposed to it; the Herodians were quite happy with the existing situation as they benefited by their support of Herod Antipas. Here then we have two parties opposed to each other on this and many other subjects uniting temporarily in order to overthrow Jesus.

If Christ had said it was lawful to pay Roman taxes, the Pharisees would have denounced him in front of the people. On the other hand, if Christ had said the taxes were not lawful, he would be immediately in trouble with the Romans. His answer is skilful: pay to Caesar what is due to him; pay to God (the Temple) what is due to him.

The question about life after death

Mark **12**, 18-27
Matt. **22**, 23-33
Luke **20**, 27-40

The Pharisees having failed to upset Jesus, the Sadducees make a further effort, this time to ridicule his teaching about the after-life. In Deuteronomy **25** the law of Moses states, 'When brothers live

c*

together and one of them dies without leaving a son, his widow shall not marry outside the family. Her husband's brother shall take her in marriage and do his duty by her as her husband's brother,' in order to produce a son who shall take his dead brother's name and be his heir. The Sadducees then put to Jesus an absurd situation which they thought could arise in the after-life, in the existence of which they did not believe. Christ replied that the after-life is spiritual in character and marriage as we know it does not exist. He also quotes the Scriptures against their unbelief in the future life. If Abraham's existence had ceased at death, God would no longer be the God of Abraham, but only of his earthly remains, which was absurd. God said 'I am the God of Abraham', not 'I was'.

The greatest commandment

Mark 12, 28-34
Matt. 22, 34-40

The lawyer asking the question is not hostile to Jesus. Jesus replies by quoting the words of the Shema which were repeated daily by the Jews. He adds a second commandment from Leviticus 19, 18. To a Jew the word 'neighbour' meant a fellow Jew. Jesus interprets it to mean any human being (cf., the parable of the good Samaritan, Luke 10).

The parable of the wicked husbandmen

Mark 12, 1-12
Matt. 21, 33-46
Luke 20, 9-19

Christ clearly implies here that he is Messiah. Every detail fits. The vineyard represented the Jewish nation; the owner's servants, the former prophets; the husbandmen, the Jewish rulers and teachers; and the owner's son, the Messiah. Rejected finally by them, Messiah will found a new community to inherit God's kingdom.

The parable of the two sons

Matt. 21, 28-32

The Scribes and Pharisees pay lip service only. They say 'I go' but do no work for God. Many tax-collectors and prostitutes on the other hand, rejected God at first but now are keen followers of Christ.

The parables of the marriage feast and the great banquet

Matt. 22, 1-14
Luke 14, 15-24

The two parables are intended to teach similar lessons. The Jews pictured a great banquet as a symbol of Messiah's coming rule. In Matthew we have a marriage feast, (accepted later by Christians as a symbol of Christ's union with his Church). The invitation to the Jewish people to enter his Kingdom was largely despised by them. It went therefore to others - gentiles and outcasts.

The addition by Matthew of the incident of the man without wedding clothes may have once been a separate story, since people brought in to a feast unexpectedly might not have the opportunity to dress properly. The incident symbolises in another form contempt for the master of the house.

The parable of the ten virgins

Matt. 25, 1-13
The custom was for the bridegroom to fetch the bride in a triumphal procession from her home to his. The parable may refer to Christ's second coming. In any case, it teaches watchfulness. The Jews had not prepared themselves for Messiah's coming. Be prepared, Jesus was saying, for you cannot know at what hour you will have to give an account of your life.

The parables of the talents and the pounds

Matt. 25, 14-30
Luke 19, 11-27
Mark 4, 25
Both these parables have to do with the same subject as the parable of the ten virgins - a time of reckoning. In the story of the talents each man is given a different amount of money according to his ability; in the story of the pounds, each man is given the same sum. The question each has to answer, whether we are to apply the parables to the Jewish nation as a whole or to individuals, is simply 'What have you done with the abilities and opportunities that God has given you?'

The final judgment

Matt. 25, 31-46
In a strikingly symbolic form Jesus here paints an unforgettable picture of the day of reckoning. 'All nations' must, it seems, be restricted to all men who have heard the gospel, since those who have never heard of Jesus can hardly be judged by his standards.

It is what people do, rather than what they say, that matters (cf., the two houses, Matt. 7, 24-27). These words of Christ have inspired Christians in every generation to be in the vanguard of social reform and to send out missions of teaching and healing all over the known world.

Is Messiah David's son?

Mark 12, 35-37
Matt. 22, 41-46
Luke 20, 41-44
This is an academic argument aimed at the Scribes. It may have been inspired by Christ's irritation at the narrow view they held of Messiah's character. Messiah was not to be a second David in the sense of a fighting liberator of the nation.

The Widow's mite Mark 12, 41-44 Luke 21, 1-4	Christ is in the Women's Court of the Temple, where thirteen trumpet-shaped brass chests of the Treasury stood. The widow puts in a very small coin. Christ points out the real meaning of sacrifice, not giving merely what one can spare, as the rich often do.

Prophecy of Jerusalem's destruction and the Second Coming

Mark 13, 1-37 Matt. 24, 1-44 Luke 21, 5-38	Apocalypse, the Greek word meaning revelation, is applied to many passages in the Bible that describe prophetic visions. For example, the last book of the New Testament, Revelation, is known as the Apocalypse, since the whole of it is concerned with symbolic visions of future events.

The passages that we are now studying are apocalyptic. They are full of symbolism, some of which Christ took from the Old Testament. Dramatic descriptions such as the stars falling from heaven and the Son of Man coming in clouds with great power and glory may not have been intended literally at all but as a symbolic way of describing the end of earthly life as we know it and the final triumph over evil of the goodness and love of God.

These are the three subjects dealt with: the fall of Jerusalem, the persecution of Christ's followers and the Second Coming.

The Temple in Jerusalem was much admired. The wonderful stones referred to were great marble blocks 11.5m by 3.75m by 5m. The building was begun in 20 B.C. and not completed until A.D. 64. Many Jewish teachers argued that it was indestructible and therefore Judaism could never be destroyed.

But Christ's prophecy was correct. In A.D. 70 the Roman general, Titus, overthrew the city and left the Tenth Legion behind to demolish the Temple. It was set on fire, the remains demolished, and the land on which it was built ploughed up.

The 'sacrilege' or 'abomination of desolation' referred to in Matthew and Mark may have been the Roman Standards worshipped by the army, set up in the Temple. Jerusalem was packed with Passover visitors and the suffering of the people was very great. According to the Jewish historian, Josephus, there were many false messiahs and prophets at this time who led the people out into the wilderness. One company of 6000 perished there.

Christ prophesied that before the fall of Jerusalem his followers would suffer great persecution. This too happened and as Mark's gospel was available in Rome about the time of Nero's horrible persecution of Christians, Christ's words of encouragement recorded here would be a great comfort to them.

The prophecy of the Second Coming which follows is difficult mainly because it implies that Christ's return is to be expected very soon. We know that the early church believed this. Whether Jesus himself believed it (he confessed that only his Father knew the day and the hour, Mark, 13, 32), or whether the statement that this generation would see all this happen refers only to the fall of Jerusalem, we do not know. That Jesus believed that the Second Coming was near is supported by his answer to the High Priest at his trial (Mark 14, 62).

The plot to destroy Christ

Mark **14**, 1, 2, 10 11
Matt. **26**, 14-16
     27, 3-10
Luke **22**, 1-6

No satisfactory explanation of Judas's betrayal has ever been suggested. The amount of money offered was trivial. Was it that Judas wanted to force Christ's hand, with all the people behind him to declare himself as God's conquering Messiah and liberate his chosen people forever? When we think of how the disciples quarrelled about the positions they would hold in the New Kingdom, this may possibly be the answer, and would account for Judas's later disillusionment and suicide. Alternately, since Jesus's messiahship was obviously a disaster and his enemies were gradually closing in on him, did Judas decide to desert to his enemies for his own safety?

The anointing of Christ

Mark **14**, 3-9
Matt. **26**, 1-13

Simon the leper, if he was present, had clearly been cured of his leprosy. The home in Bethany that Jesus visited on a number of occasions was that of Mary, Martha and their brother, Lazarus. Was this the same house and Simon possibly the father? In John **12**, 1-8 we have a similar story in which Mary anoints Christ and Judas objects to the waste of money. Kings were anointed as also were dead bodies prepared for burial.

Preparation for the Last Supper

Mark **14**, 12-16
Matt. **26**, 17-19
Luke **22**, 7-13

The Passover in this year coincided with the Sabbath. Rather than eat the Passover meal on the Sabbath some Jews would eat it on the previous evening. This, Jesus was evidently doing and the Last Supper held on the Thursday night was also for him and his disciples the Passover meal.

A man carrying a water pot as described in Mark and Matthew would attract attention. Women usually did this work. The house was possibly that of John Mark's mother used later as a regular meeting place for the disciples.

The Last Supper
Mark 14, 17-31
Matt. **26**, 20-35
Luke **22**, 14-38

As the Passover meal proceeds, Jesus uses the unleavened bread and the wine to institute a solemn ceremony which has, in Christ's spiritual presence, been carried on by his followers ever since. It is known variously as the Holy Communion, The Eucharist, The Sacrament of the Lord's Supper, The Mass, The Breaking of Bread.

Blessing the bread Jesus passed it to his disciples saying, 'This is my body' (Luke adds, 'which is given for you; this do in remembrance of me'). Then taking the wine he gave it to them saying, 'This is my blood of the (new) covenant, which is poured out for many'.

The two words, 'blood' and 'covenant', would immediately link this action in the minds of the disciples with the Old Covenant that God made with their forefathers through Moses, and which they had failed to keep (Exodus **24**, 1-8). God was evidently now offering them a New Covenant or contract. Christ's sacrifice of himself in death, like the sacrifice of the lamb recorded in Exodus, would symbolise forever God's forgiveness for the past and the new life he now offered them for the future.

This would account for why Jesus believed that his death was necessary and was prophesied in the Old Testament (possibly Isaiah **53**).

Notice the disciples', and especially Peter's, rather pathetic vows of loyalty to him. In Luke we have a passage (**22**, 24-28) teaching humility and service as essential to a Christian, and in v. 35-38 a remarkable suggestion that all kinds of resources might be necessary to preserve the Christian faith against its most bitter enemies. Perhaps only the fact that the disciples were armed enabled them to escape the violent mob in Gethsemane.

Gethsemane
Mark 14, 32-52
Matt. **26**, 36-56
Luke **22**, 39-53

Gethsemane was a tree-covered garden on the slopes of the Mount of Olives, which according to the Fourth Gospel, Jesus and his disciples had often visited. It would be well known to Judas.

The three disciples, Peter, James and John, having seen Jesus not many weeks previously in a heavenly setting in his transfiguration now saw his human side as he wrestled in prayer to avoid the terrible ordeal awaiting him.

The young man mentioned in Mark was quite possibly John Mark himself. Judas would bring the Temple soldiers and the mob to the upper room where the Last Supper took place. If this was the home of Mark's mother, it is likely that John Mark would leap from his bed hastily in an attempt to reach Jesus in Gethsemane first in order to warn him of the approach of the mob.

Questions for revision

1. Describe Christ's entry into Jerusalem and his cleansing of the Temple. Why did these two events make it more necessary and yet more difficult for the authorities to take some action against Christ?
2. Give an account of the three main questions put to Jesus by the Jewish leaders during Holy Week and his answers to them. Point out the importance of both questions and answers in each case.
3. Write all you know about Judas Iscariot. Can you offer any explanation of his behaviour?

Trial, Crucifixion and Resurrection

Note that in the following columns, under MARK you have Mark's story in note form with some minor additions by Matthew in the 'Trial' and 'Crucifixion', but in the other columns *only the additions* to the Markan story that each gospel gives.

The Trial

It is common to speak of two trials, the first before Caiaphas and the Sanhedrin and the second before Pilate. The trial before Caiaphas, however, must have been more in the nature of a preliminary enquiry before the Roman trial, since by Jewish law, a man on a capital charge must be tried during daylight hours; his trial must last at least two days if a verdict of 'guilty' is to be given; and sentence must be postponed until the day after the verdict is given. This was ancient Jewish law.

Whether under the Romans the Jews were allowed to put people to death is doubtful. In John's gospel the Jews say to Pilate 'It is not lawful for us to put any man to death' (John **18**, 31) and the death of Stephen and the attempted murder of Christ when he returned to Nazareth are surely only examples of mob violence.

Note that Jesus was condemned before the Sanhedrin for blasphemy. Three charges were made against him before Pilate (see Luke's account) but in John it seems that the crucial issue was whether Jesus was in opposition to Caesar. 'If you release this man, you are not Caesar's friend; everyone who makes himself a King sets himself against Caesar,' said the Jews to Pilate.

Pilate could not afford to ignore criticism of this kind. He had been repremanded once already by the Emperor for his treatment of the Jews. Further, it was very important to pacify the Jews during the Passover festival. Counting inhabitants and pilgrims there would be more than two million people swarming in and around Jerusalem, and if their leaders were angry and dissatisfied there could be turbulence, if not open rebellion, in the capital. Pilate as a minor official - a mere procurator - had only 3000 troops with which to keep the peace. He was almost bound to satisfy the High Priest's demands.

The Trial

MARK
14, 53 - 16, 20
Matt. 26, 57 - 27, 31

Christ led to the Council Chamber (of the Sanhedrin). Peter follows and warms himself by the fire.

Before Caiaphas, the witnesses do not agree even on the rebuilding of the Temple. Jesus confesses that he is the Messiah, 'The Son of God', and that they will see him again after death. They spit on him.and buffet him. Peter denies Christ. After consultations Christ is taken to Pilate.

Before Pilate Christ is asked if he is King of the Jews. He agrees but says no more. Matthew adds that Pilate's wife beseeched him to release Christ, and that before the crowd Pilate washed his hands in an endeavour to absolve himself from blame.

Pilate offers the people Christ or Barabbas. Pilate releases Barabbas and delivers Christ for scourging and crucifixion. The soldiers make sport with him in the Praetorium.

LUKE
22, 54 - 23, 25

Servants kindle a fire and a maid recognises Peter by the light of it. Two other people also accuse him. After his third denial Christ 'turned and looked at Peter'.

The Jewish Council is held in the morning.

Before Pilate the Jews accuse Christ of stirring up the people, of forbidding tax paying and saying that he is the Messiah. Pilate sends Christ to Herod since he is a Galilean. Herod wishes to see a miracle but Christ does nothing. Herod's soldiers mock him. Herod and Pilate become friends. Pilate argues again with the Jews - Christ had done no evil. Pilate releases Barabbas and delivers Christ for crucifixion.

JOHN
18, 12 - 19, 16

Peter and John follow Christ and through John's influence enter the Court.

Before Annas, Christ is asked about his teaching. Christ's reply to Annas provokes an officer to strike the prisoner. Christ is now sent to Caiaphas.

A relative of Malchus says to Peter, 'Did I not see thee in the garden?' Christ is taken to Pilate.

Before Pilate. The Jews will not enter the Palace. Pilate is not satisfied with their accusations. They should judge him themselves. They reply that they cannot put him to death. Note Pilate's examination of Christ:
1. Art thou King of the Jews?
2. Art thou a King?
3. Whence art thou?
Pilate is afraid. He offers Barabbas. Pilate scourges Christ and brings him out wearing a purple robe and a crown of thorns. 'Behold the man.' The Jews reply 'He made himself the Son of God'. Pilate examines Christ again. He brings Christ out to 'the pavement'. 'Behold your King'. They reply, 'We have no king but Caesar. If you release this man you are not Caesar's Friend'. This decides Pilate who gives in to the Jews.

The Crucifixion

MARK
15, 21-47
Matt. 27, 32-66

Simon of Cyrene compelled to take the cross to Golgotha, the Place of a Skull.

Christ is offered myrrh and wine. The soldiers cast lots for his garments. It was the third hour. The superscription: 'The King of the Jews'. The two thieves. The spectators and the Chief Priests scoff at him, 'Save thyself and come down from the Cross.'

There is darkness between the sixth and ninth hours. Jesus cries, *'My God, my God, why hast thou forsaken me?'* The bystanders think he is calling for Elijah. Vinegar is offered him. Jesus cries with a loud voice and dies. The curtain of the Temple is torn. The centurion: 'Truly this man was the Son of God.' (Matt: tombs opened and bodies of the saints appeared in Jerusalem.) The women present. Joseph of Arimathea claims the body from Pilate. Pilate confirms that he is dead. The body is placed in a tomb, the position of which the women observe. (Matt: Pilate agrees to the Chief Priests' request that the tomb be guarded.)

LUKE
23, 26-56

A multitude follow him. Jesus tells the women to weep rather for themselves - a reference to the destruction of Jerusalem.

Jesus says:, *'Father forgive them for they know not what they do'*. One thief rails on him, 'Save thyself and us'. The other rebukes him and says, 'Remember me when thou comest into thy Kingdom'. Christ replies, *'Today thou shalt be with me in Paradise'*.

About the ninth hour Jesus cries with a loud voice, *'Father, into thy hands I commend my spirit'*. The crowd sympathises with Christ.

Joseph of Arimathea, a councillor, had not agreed with the Sanhedrin's verdict.

The women follow the body.

JOHN
19, 17-42

The soldiers divide his garments into four parts and cast lots for his seamless coat. The superscription, written by Pilate is in Hebrew, Greek and Latin. The chief priests object to the superscription. They said it should be 'This man said "I am the King of the Jews"'. Christ points out his mother to John. *'Woman, behold thy son, Son, behold thy mother'.*

Jesus says, *'I thirst'.* he accepts vinegar and hyssop.

Jesus cries, *'It is finished'* and dies. The legs of the other prisoners are broken. a spear is plunged into Christ's side.

Nicodemus helps Joseph.

The Resurrection

MARK
16, 1-20

Mary Magdalene, Mary, mother of James and Salome bring spices with which to annoint Christ's body. Very early they arrive at the tomb. 'Who will roll away the Stone?' But the stone is rolled back. A young man in white says, 'Do not be amazed. He has risen ...go tell his disciples ...he is going before you into Galilee'. They flee in astonishment and are too amazed to tell anyone.

What follows was added to the Gospel by an unknown writer.

Christ appears to Mary Magdalene who runs to tell the disciples who disbelieve her.

He appears to two of them as they walk in the country.

He appears to the eleven at a meal. He upbraids them for their unbelief; tells them to preach the gospel and promises great power to them.

MATTHEW
28, 1-20

A great earthquake and an angel rolls away the stone and sits upon it. The guards become as dead men. Later they tell the chief priests and are given money to say that the disciples stole the body.

The women depart and Jesus meets them saying, 'Hail!' They take hold of his feet. He tells them to tell the disciples to meet him in Galilee.

He appears to the disciples on a mountain in Galilee but some doubt. Jesus tells them to go and preach the gospel. 'Lo, I am with you always'.

LUKE
24, 1-53

Mary Magdalene, Mary the mother of James and Joanna are at the tomb. Two men appear in the tomb in dazzling clothes. They remind the women of what Christ had said about his death and resurrection. The disciples when told by the women disbelieve and Peter runs to the tomb and finds the grave clothes.

Jesus appears to the two on the way to Emmaus. They do not know him till he breaks bread. They return immediately to Jerusalem and tell the others.

Jesus appears to them all. They think he is a ghost. He shows them his hands and side and eats some fish. He explains the Scriptures to them. He leads them to Bethany, blesses them and departs and they return to Jerusalem.

JOHN
20, 1 - 21, 25

Mary Magdalene, while it is yet dark, reaches the tomb. She sees the stone rolled away and runs to tell Peter and John, saying that the body has been stolen. John arrives before Peter. Both find the linen clothes and napkin. Mary Magdalene remains and sees two angels in the tomb who ask her why she weeps.

Jesus appears to Mary Magdalene, who thinks him to be the gardener. He tells her to go and tell the disciples.

Jesus appears on the Sunday evening to the disciples behind closed doors, shows his hands and side and gives them the Holy Spirit.

Jesus appears to Thomas a week later.

Jesus appears to Peter and six other disciples on the Sea of Galilee at daybreak. The miracle of the 153 fishes. A fire and Jesus gives them the fish and bread. 'Simon Peter, lovest thou me?' (three times). The fate of Peter.

Questions for revision

1. Describe the trial of Jesus before the High Priest. Why did Caiaphas want Jesus put to death? What arguments, if any could you find to justify his action?
2. (a) Describe all that happened as Jesus hung on the Cross.
   (b) Which of these happenings show us what God is like?
   (c) What meaning should the Crucifixion have for us today?
3. Describe four of Christ's resurrection appearances. What is there about Christ's appearances that is wholly different from any other ghostly stories we hear about?

Passages from the Fourth Gospel

I Passages specially connected with incidents recorded in the
   Synoptic Gospels.
   The Incarnation.
   The baptism of Jesus and the call of the disciples.
   The day after the feeding of the five thousand and Peter's
      confession.
   The Greeks seek Jesus.
   The Last Supper.

II Some other important events.
    The first miracle.
    Nicodemus.
    The woman of Samaria.
    The lame man of Bethesda.
    The man born blind.
    The raising of Lazarus.

The Incarnation
John 1, 1-14

Matthew and Luke each have their own way of describing the
coming of Christ into the world - the Incarnation. John's description is the most difficult because it is strongly influenced by the
philosophical ideas of the period.

His opening words remind us of the Creation story (Genesis 1).
He draws a parallel between the Creation and the coming of
Christ.

'The Word', which is used frequently in this passage, may be
thought of as meaning the Mind and Power of God - a combin-
ation of Greek and Hebrew ideas. It is specially related here to
Jesus Christ who was with God and indeed was God from the
beginning of time (see Christ's striking answer to the Pharisees:
'Before Abraham was, I am.' John 8, 58).

In Genesis the first act of the Word was the creation of light
and the separation of the darkness from it. In the Gospel the first
act was the bringing of a new spiritual light to mankind when
'the Word became flesh and dwelt among us' in the person of
Jesus Christ.

He brought also a new creation which the synoptic writers call
the Kingdom of God, and those who accepted the Light entered

the Kingdom and became the Children of God. So men could enter into an entirely new relationship with God which was to supersede the ancient belief that the Jews were God's chosen people because they were the Children of Abraham. Note what John the Baptist has to say about this claim in Matthew 3, 8 and 9.

The baptism of Jesus and the call of the disciples.

John 1, 29-51   The Fourth Gospel does not describe the baptism of Jesus but only what John the Baptist said about it afterwards. He asserts that he recognised Christ by seeing 'the Spirit descend as a dove from heaven' and rest upon him. Mark declares that Jesus alone had this vision. At the time of Passover a lamb was sacrificed and John's reference to Jesus as the Lamb of God is a comparison of Christ's sacrifice and death with that of the Passover lamb.

The incident of Simon and Andrew meeting Jesus, given in v. 35 onwards, must have taken place before their encounter with him while fishing on the shores of the Sea of Galilee. Here we are told they recognise him as the Messiah and Jesus renames Simon, Cephas, a name given to him according to Matthew at Caesarea Philippi. In trying to reconcile these different accounts it may be noted that a previous meeting with Jesus would explain the suddenness with which Simon and Andrew were later prepared to leave their fishing and become his disciples.

Nathanial does not appear in the Synoptics but he may possibly be identified with Bartholomew. Simon and Andrew came from Capernaum according to Mark, not Bethsaida.

The day after the feeding of the five thousand. Peter's confession

John 6, 22-71   Part of this discourse of Jesus took place by the seaside and the rest in the synagogue in Capernaum. It is important because it deals in detail with what happened the day after the feeding of the five thousand. Many of those whom Jesus had fed crossed the Sea of Galilee to find him, though they were perplexed to discover that he was in Capernaum, not knowing how he had crossed the sea.

He tells them that they have come to him because he fed them, but they should really be seeking spiritual not material food. In reply the people declare that the manna Moses gave their fore-fathers in the wilderness was a sign from God that Moses was their God-chosen leader. What sign would Jesus give them?

Jesus replies that he is the true and eternal manna - the Bread of Life. It is God's purpose that he should come into the world to

74

save to eternity everyone who accepted him. Their forefathers who ate the manna in the wilderness died, but those who eat his flesh and drink his blood shall have eternal life.

The Jews are deeply offended by what Jesus says, believing him to be merely the son of the carpenter, Joseph of Nazareth. Many of his followers also leave him. He appeals to his disciples: 'Will you also go away?' But Peter replies, 'Lord, to whom shall we go? You have the words of eternal life.' (This reply of Peter's is the counterpart in the Fourth Gospel to Peter's Confession in Caesarea Philippi recorded in the Synoptics - see Matt. **16**, 13-20.)

Holy Week
John 12, 20-36

The Greeks
This incident is important because it seems to end Christ's public teaching. It takes place on the Wednesday within forty-eight hours of his death.

The Greeks referred to here are Gentiles who had accepted the Jewish faith and are called by the Jews 'proselytes of the gate', from the passage in the Old Testament that speaks of 'the sojourner within your gates' (Ex. **20**, 10). They may have come from Bethsaida or from one of the Greek cities of Decapolis.

In reply to the Greeks' request Jesus speaks to the crowd around him. The time has now come, he implies, for him to act rather than to speak; his death and resurrection will speak for themselves to the whole Gentile world.

Compare the fear Jesus feels as he contemplates the terrible ordeal of his death with his prayer in Gethsemane (Mark **14**, 32-36).

John 13, 1-19

Jesus washes his disciples' feet
Ever since Jesus at Caesarea Philippi had revealed himself as Messiah, the disciples increasingly looked forward to the great kingdom on earth that he would establish. They argued continually among themselves about the various positions they would hold in that kingdom and who among them would be the greatest. Even the solemn atmosphere of the Last Supper was disturbed by their quarrelling (Luke **22**, 24-27).

It seems that Jesus, now in despair that all his teaching on service and humility remained unheeded, decided that only the dramatic action of washing their feet would drive home once and for all the true meaning of discipleship.

John **15**, 26   *Christ promises the gift of the Holy Spirit*
John **16**, 7-14   When finally the disciples realised that Jesus was about to leave
John **14**, 16-28   them, they were very downcast, but he promised that the Holy
                     Spirit would come to them as a comforter, counsellor and
                     advocate (Acts **2**) and would stand by them in every situation
                     however difficult.
                        He taught that the Holy Spirit would:
                     1. Make up for his absence.
                     2. Ensure that they would remember his teaching.
                     3. Reveal clearly, as the spirit of truth, what was good and what
                        was evil in the world.
                     4. Make plain to them the meaning of the crucifixion and resur-
                        rection and teach them whatever else they would need to know.
                     5. Exalt Christ in the world.
                     6. Give them peace in trouble and words with which to defend
                        themselves before their enemies.

                     Christ's discourses
                     Also in the Fourth Gospel it is recorded how Jesus talked at length
                     to the disciples round the supper table. These discourses contain
                     some of his most memorable sayings as, for example,
                        'I am the Vine, you are the branches. He who abides in me and
                        I in him, he it is that bears much fruit.' John **15**, 5.
                        'Greater love has no man than this, that a man lay down his life
                        for his friends.' John **15**, 13.
                        'Let not your hearts be troubled. . . . I go to prepare a place
                        for you and I will come again and take you to myself that
                        where I am there you may be also.' John **14**, 1-3.
                        'I am the Way and the Truth and the Life, no one comes to the
                        Father but by me.' John **14**, 6.
                        'He who has seen me has seen the Father.' John **14**, 9.
                        Chapters **13** - **17** give a deep insight into the spiritual meaning
                     of the gospel. It is probably better to read chapter 14 after chapter
                     17 as it seems to contain Christ's final words to his disciples (see
                     14, v. 31).

The first miracle   At first sight, this miracle may appear trivial, since most of Christ's
John **2**, 1-11   other miracles are performed to relieve acute human distress. In
                    fact, it seems that Jesus himself was at first uncertain as to how he
                    should act in these circumstances, though his mother had no
                    doubts. However, one has to realise that for most women

(especially in Christ's day) their wedding was the most important event in their lives. To find that in the middle of the celebrations the guests are not properly provided for would be a catastrophe, an embarrassing occasion remembered for the rest of one's life. This certainly would be no trivial incident for the bride and bridegroom in Cana.

Christ's reply to his mother has been variously translated. The Greek text is brief (five words) and ambiguous. Perhaps the best translation is that of the New English Bible: 'Your concern, Mother, is not mine.'

Six stone jars would hold 545-828 litres but from a careful reading of the text it does not follow that Christ produced 828 litres of wine.

Miracles in the Fourth Gospel are described as 'signs', signs of the wonder and joy to be found within the Kingdom of God.

Nicodemus
John 3, 1-21

Usually, according to the Fourth Gospel, when Jesus is in Jerusalem he is facing bitter criticism from the authorities. This incident - the first of three involving Nicodemus - is a welcome change. Nicodemus is a member of the Jewish Council, the Sanhedrin, and is recognised as an honoured teacher of the Law.

He addresses Jesus as 'Rabbi' and confesses that his fellow Scribes recognise Jesus as a teacher from God because he performs such astonishing miracles. Yet obviously they did not share his sympathetic interest in Jesus, otherwise he would not have found it necessary to visit him at night-time.

Christ's teaching here is about the need of being born a second time - a new birth in which a man knows unmistakeably the presence of God's spirit within him. The phrase 'to be born of water' may refer to a baptism of repentance or simply to a natural birth.

Jesus speaks here of the Judgment, usually thought of as at the end of life, as having already begun. Men judge themselves by accepting the Light or rejecting it. Salvation therefore requires not only a baptism of the Spirit but good works that will bear the light of Christ's scrutiny.

The passage also contains a famous verse (16) in which the essence of the Gospel is summed up.

Note that Nicodemus makes an attempt later to support Jesus in a debate in the Sanhedrin (7, 50-52) and after his death joins with Joseph of Arimathea in looking after his body when it has been taken down from the cross (19, 39).

The woman of Samaria

John 4, 1-42   What is specially important to note in this story is Christ's interest in and concern for Samaritans. A strict Jew travelling from Judaea to Galilee would not set foot in Samaria because of the traditional enmity between the two people, Jesus not only passes through Samaria but actually holds a conversation with a Samaritan woman. A Jewish rabbi would not normally hold a conversation with a woman if he could avoid it. This then is another of many occasions when Jesus shows concern to help and teach non-Jews, though he makes it clear to the woman that salvation comes through the Jewish race. It is a remarkable example of Christ's powers that after only two days in Samaria as a teacher from a hostile race he converts so many of them to a belief in him as Messiah.

That, as Jesus says, one will sow (the seed of the Gospel) and another will reap will happen increasingly on the vast missionary field of Christianity, beginning here in Samaria.

The lame man of Bethesda

John 5, 1-18   The incident is notable for three ways in which Jesus deeply offends the Jewish leaders. First, he heals a man on the Sabbath, then he causes the man himself to break the Sabbath by telling him to carry his bed, and then finally he makes himself equal with God.

Whatever laws the Jews had about no work on the Sabbath, it was always a matter for discussion among the rabbis as to what work God did on the seventh day. Since the Jews maintained that God not only created the universe but sustained it day by day, it was obvious that the Sabbath could not be for him a day of complete rest. Jesus assumed this, declaring that since God, his Father, worked on the Sabbath, he too had a right to work on that day. This claim of equality with God infuriated his critics and they determined to kill him.

Note Christ's final advice to the man whom he healed not to sin any more lest a worse fate befel him. Is Jesus here linking the man's disease with some sin he has commited, as he did possibly with the paralysed man? (Mark 2, 1-12.)

The man born blind

John 9, 1-41   Verse 3 makes us realise that the following incident is a very exceptional one. By the manner in which Jesus throughout his ministry worked long hours - often it seems at high speed - to relieve physical suffering, we might conclude that suffering was not the will of God. Yet here Jesus implies that this man may have been born blind in order that what Jesus says and does in giving him sight may be seen and remembered always.

The story itself needs little comment. We should note the power of the Pharisees and the justifiable fear of them by the common people. They could excommunicate, that is, exclude anyone from the synagogue (v. 22). In such a society that exclusion could cause disgrace and suffering beyond measure. Notice, too, how the young man's faultless argument confounds the Pharisees so that they can do nothing else but abuse him. He presents them again with their perpetual dilemma: Jesus cannot have come from the devil because of his good works.

Verses 39-41 drive home the real meaning behind this acted parable. Those who recognise their spiritual blindness Jesus can give sight to, but those who think or pretend they can see actually remain blind and nothing can be done for them.

The raising of Lazarus
John 11, 1-44

This is the third occasion on which Jesus brings to life someone who has died. The other two are the widow of Nain's son (Luke 7, 11-17) and Jairus's daughter (Mark 5, 21-42). It is probably the most important because there is no question of death not having taken place (cf., Jairus's daughter). There was a curious belief that the soul lingered about the body for three days after death. Lazarus had been dead four days. Another important factor is that the report of this sign or miracle to the High Priest and the Sanhedrin made them all the more determined to destroy Jesus on whatever pretext they could find. Finally, the occasion is important because of the teaching Jesus gives about himself when talking to Martha.

From v. 4 it seems that Jesus had some foreknowledge of what was going to happen, though his delay in going to Bethany would not be in order to perform a greater miracle but to complete the work he was engaged upon. Martha and Mary have already been introduced to us in the gospel story (Luke 10, 38-42) though there has been no mention of Lazarus.

Notice that in his prayer before the open tomb Jesus is very anxious to rebut the assertion by his enemies that his power did not come from God.

The most memorable teaching on this occasion is to be found in v. 25, 26;

'I am the resurrection and the life; he who believes in me,

though he die, yet shall he live, and whoever lives and believes in me shall never die.'

Revision questions on the Fourth Gospel

Pages 10-12 should also be read before answering these questions.

1. What were the main reasons for enmity between the Jews and S Samaritans? Show how Jesus ignored them in his encounter with the woman of Samaria and the success he achieved. On what other occasion recorded in the Synoptic Gospels did a Samaritan show appreciation of what Jesus did?

2. List the 'signs' that Jesus gave of his power which are recorded in John's gospel. Describe fully the occasion of the first one. Why do you think Jesus hesitated before he performed this miracle?

3. Describe briefly the important additions to the story of the Last Supper that the Fourth Gospel gives us.

4. (a) Show in what way John's treatment of the Incarnation differs from the account in the Synoptic Gospels.
   (b) What evidence is there that the writer had Genesis I in mind when he wrote it?
   (c) In the Fourth Gospel Jesus refers to himself as the Light of the World, and in the Synoptic Gospels to his disciples as the Light of the World. What were the occasions?

5. Give an account of the occasion and the crisis that followed when Jesus described himself as the Bread of Life.

6. Imagine yourself as one of the Pharisees to whom the man who was born blind was brought. Describe what happened and explain why in the end you threw the man out.

7. In the Fourth Gospel what words does Jesus use in place of 'The Kingdom of God'? Describe the notable occasion when Jesus referred to himself as 'The Resurrection and the Life'.

8. Describe Christ's encounter with a friendly Pharisee. Outline briefly what he taught him. How did it affect the later behaviour of the Pharisee?

List of Christ's Miracles

List of Christ's Parables

Most of Christ's parables are about the Kingdom of God in its present or final form. The first eleven parables listed here begin with an immediate comparison such as 'The Kingdom of God is like. . . . '

	Parable	*Bible reference*	*Teaching*
32	The seed growing secretly	Mark 4, 26-29	The secret growth of the Kingdom.
37	The mustard seed	Luke 13, 18-19	The rapid growth of the Kingdom.
		Mark 4, 30-32	
		Matt. 13, 31-32	
37	The leaven	Luke 13, 20	The rapid growth of the Kingdom.
		Matt. 13, 33	
37	The wheat and the weeds	Matt. 13, 24-30	Both good and evil flower until the Judgement Day.
		36-43	
37	The dragnet	Matt. 13, 47-50	Both good and evil flower until Judgment Day.
37	The treasure	Matt. 13, 44	The Kingdom is worth more than everything else.
37	The pearl	Matt. 13, 45-46	
56	The unmerciful servant	Matt. 18, 23-34	Forgiveness.
63	The ten virgins	Matt. 25, 1-13	Watchfulness.
58	The labourers in the vineyard	Matt. 20, 1-16	God's generosity - the Kingdom is a gift.
62	The marriage feast	Matt. 22, 1-10	The Jews' rejection of Christ; other accept him.
31	The sower	Mark 4, 1-9	The different ways in which people react to the Gospel.
		13-20	
		Luke 8, 4-8	
		11-15	
		Matt. 13, 1-9	
		18-23	
41	The importunate neighbour	Luke 11, 5-8	Perseverance in prayer.
43	The two houses	Luke 6, 47-49	The importance of doing what Christ teaches us.
		Matt. 7, 24-27	
45	The good Samaritan	Luke 10, 25-37	To love one's neighbour.
47	The faithful servants	Luke 12, 35-40	Watchfulness.
47	The faithful steward	Matt. 24, 45-51	Faithful service.
		Luke 12, 41-48	

Page	Parable	Bible reference	Teaching
47	The rich fool	Luke 12, 13-21	Warning against avarice.
48	The fruitless fig tree	Luke 13, 6-9	Need for repentance and good works.
49	The tower and the king going to war	Luke 14, 28-33	Counting the cost of discipleship.
49	The lost sheep	Matt. 18, 12-14 Luke 15, 1-7	God's concern for sinners.
49	The lost coin	Luke 15, 8-10	
49	The prodigal son	Luke 15, 11-32	
49	The unjust steward	Luke 16, 1-9	To be 'wise as serpents'
50	The rich man and Lazarus	Luke 16, 19-31	Wealth used selfishly is condemned.
50	The unprofitable servant	Luke 17, 7-10	The Kingdom is a gift - we cannot earn it.
51	The unjust judge	Luke 18, 1-8	Perseverance in prayer.
51	The Pharisee and the publican.	Luke 18, 9-14	Humility in prayer.
62	The wicked husbandmen	Mark 12, 1-12 Matt. 21, 33-46 Luke 20, 9-19	The Jew's rejection of Christ.
62	The two sons	Matt. 21, 28-32	The 'righteous' reject Christ; the sinners repent.
62	The great banquet	Luke 14, 15-24	The Jews' rejection of Christ; others accept him.
63	The talents	Matt. 25, 14-30	To use the gifts that God has given us.
63	The pounds	Luke 19, 11-27	

Appendix

Though the teaching of Jesus is in simple language and often in story form, it is not easy to summarise because in the Gospels it is not arranged in any convenient order.

In this appendix you will find short summaries under subject headings of some of his more important teaching and the problems he had to face.

Christ's teaching about the Kingdom of God

The Kingdom of God, or as it is called in Matthew, the Kingdom of Heaven, was the principal subject of Christ's teaching.

The title was not a new one. The Jews expected a Messiah sent by God to deliver them from their oppressors (in Christ's day, the Romans) and to lead them to victory and the fulfilment of the promises made by God to Abraham. He would probably be a warrior king, a second David, and he would establish a kingdom of wealth and plenty. This idea was apparently always at the back of his disciples' minds, since they argued - and quarrelled - about the positions they would have in the new kingdom.

Christ, however, taught that the Kingdom would be a spiritual one. 'My Kingdom is not of this world', he told Pilate, indicating that it did not consist of territory and armies to defend it. It might be more accurately described as the 'Reign of God' for it existed wherever a man allowed God to rule his life.

It was the gift of God; no one could earn it (cf., the parables of the hired labourers and the unprofitable servant). Christ offered it as a new agreement (Covenant) made with him super-seding the Old Agreement made by God with Abraham. It was worth more than everything else in life (cf., parables of the hidden treasure and the pearl).

It should be thought of in two different ways. (a) it is present in the world now - wherever God reigns. 'It is within you', he told the Pharisees. It comes as a result of repentance and faith (cf., Christ and Nicodemus). Certain parables represent the Kingdom as present in the world: The sower, the mustard seed, the leaven, the seed growing secretly. (b) It is continued in the life to come, and will take its final form when Christ returns to the world - the Second Coming. Parables illustrating this Final Judgment are the wheat and the tares, the dragnet, the talents, the pounds, the wise and foolish virgins and the great supper.

Conditions of entry into God's Kingdom involved (a) a recognition that one's past life was completely unsatisfactory (repentance) and (b) a willingness to accept, with the simple trust of a child, the guidance of God, and the saving power of Christ.

Christ's teaching about humility

Christ was continually distressed by the pride and self-satisfaction of the religious teachers of his day. An outstanding example of this, which had angered him at the beginning of his ministry, was their condescending attitude to John the Baptist. They treated Christ in much the same manner. Proud of their own way of life they had no wish to learn anything from him, (one exception being Nicodemus). They flaunted their superiority before the common people by their extravagant dress, their public show of piety and their claim to privilege.

Christ's disciples in a lesser degree suffered from a similar weakness. They were continually arguing among themselves about the high positions they would soon occupy in Christ's Kingdom.

In complete contrast to this Jesus taught that his followers should not seek prominence and power - at least not for their own sake. They should rather look at their own failings and not judge those of other people. Note the parable of the Pharisee and the publican (Luke 18, 9-14). Unlike the Pharisees they were to pray, give alms and fast without drawing attention to themselves. Those who sought 'the chief seats' should remember that 'the last shall be first and the first last'.

In the Sermon on the Mount he declared that it was the meek - the opposite of the arrogant and self-centred - who would inherit the earth.

He constantly took his disciples to task for arguing about who should be greatest in the Kingdom of God. Finally, it seems in exasperation at their desire for prominence, he acted a parable. Before the Last Supper he took upon himself the task of the most menial household servant and washed their feet. 'If I then your Lord and Teacher, have washed your feet you also ought to wash one another's feet. For I have given you an example that you should do as I have done to you.' (John 13, 14-15).

Christ's teaching about Forgiveness

Jewish law allowed exact compensation for injruy: 'an eye for an eye and a tooth for a tooth' (lex talionis). In Christ's day the Jews, who were closely bound together struggling for survival in the middle of a hostile world, thought of the word 'neighbour' as meaning a fellow Jew. Gentiles were certainly not neighbours. They were sometimes referred to as 'dogs' (cf., Mark 7, 27). From the Pharisees point of view many of their own people were excluded too: those who made no effort to keep the Law, such as tax-collectors and prostitutes, and those whose occupation kept them from synagogue, such as shepherds.

Christ taught:

1. The equality of all men. There was to be no restriction on the word 'neighbour'. Notice in this connection his healings among Gentiles, the Gerasene demoniac, the Greek woman's daughter, the centurion's servant; and his parables, especially the one about the good Samaritan.

2. That we should love our enemies. Note here that the Greek word used here for 'Love' means to 'respect'. Retaliation and revenge are not allowed, nor is returning evil for evil. 'If anyone strikes you on the right cheek, turn to him the other also and if anyone would sue you and take your coat let him have your cloak as well'. (Matt. 5, 39, 40).

3. That among Christians if a man sins against you there were four steps to be taken:
   (a) to approach him yourself
   (b) then with friends
   (c) to bring the matter before the church council or congregation and, if all this finally failed
   (d) to take him to court. (Matt. 18, 15-17).

4. That our forgiveness should be unlimited. The Pharisees taught three times; Peter suggested seven; and Christ seventy times seven (Matt. 18, 21-22).

5. That our own sins are forgiven only as we are prepared to forgive the sins of others. cf., The Lord's Prayer, the parable of the ungrateful servant, (Matt. 18, 23-35).

6. That we should be careful in our criticism and judgment of others for we are all sinners. cf., the incident of the woman taken in adultery (John 7, 53 - 8, 11) and the teaching in the Sermon on the Mount (Matt. 7, 1-5).

Christ assumed the power to forgive sins. He also set an example of forgiveness in the treatment of the Samaritans who rejected him(Luke 9, 53-56) and on the cross in forgiving his enemies (Luke 23, 34).

Christ's teaching about prayer

It is sometimes argued that the most prayer can do is to bring the person praying into touch with the mind of God and help him to accept his will. Prayer cannot interfere with the operation of natural laws and therefore cannot affect the ordinary course of events.

The whole of Christ's life and teaching assumes that the power of prayer is far greater than this. He makes it quite clear that his remarkable powers of healing both of the bodies and minds of those who came to him were the result of faith and prayer. In the gospels he is continually described as praying and as talking about the power of prayer. He lifts up his eyes to heaven before a miracle; he goes out before sunrise to pray in the countryside; he escapes to the hills to pray when tempted (after the feeding of the five thousand); he prays at length with his disciples at the Last Supper; he prays in Gethsemane and on the cross. In fact, he gives the impression that the ability to talk to God as father is the distinguishing mark of a Christian, and its effect can be revolutionary.

In the Sermon on the Mount (Matt. 6, 5-15, 7, 7-11) he teaches that:

(a) All prayer is answered. 'Ask, and it will be given you, seek, and you will find, knock, and it will be opened to you.'

We should, however, note in this context Christ's prayer in Gethsemane, 'Nevertheless, not what I will, but what thou willest, be done.' While all prayer is answered it cannot always be answered in the terms we hope for or expect.

(b) Sincere prayer is often made best in private. The Pharisees had a habit of praying in the street to impress people by their piety.

(c) The words we utter should be sincerely meant. The mere thoughtless repetition of words - as with the heathen - is useless.

(d) We should use the Lord's Prayer - praying that God's will be done, then for our fellow men and ourselves.

(e) God is anxious and willing to answer us. See in this connection the parables of the Importunate neighbour, Luke 11, 5-13 and the unjust judge, Luke 18, 1-8. Here Christ contrasts the attitude of God with that of people who care little about the needs of their fellowmen.

Christ's teaching about money

Christ was keenly aware of the inequalities in his society - the existence side by side of the very poor and the rich. He was also aware that the religious leaders of his day were generally well-to-do. In Luke 16, 14 we are told that the Pharisees were 'lovers of money' and the Sadducees were in any case very comfortably provided for (see Introduction p. 5). He himself chose the lot of a working-man.

His attitude to wealthy people does not appear as simple as that expressed in Luke 6, 24-25, where he seems to condemn the rich merely because of their wealth. It is true that he demanded of the rich young ruler that he should sell all that he had. But this may have been because he recognised that for that young man, material possessions had become his god. On the other hand, he commended the wealthy Zaccheus for making amends for his past misdeeds but did not require him to adopt a life of poverty. Christ appears to have had friends amongst both rich and poor.

Nevertheless, he insists that the dangers of wealth are immense. 'How hardly', he declares, 'shall a rich man enter the Kingdom of Heaven!' This view astonished his disciples because the Jews believed that wealth, justly acquired, was a sign of God's blessing. Christ's judgment was more penetrating. Wealth can so easily warp a man's character that it is only by God's over-ruling power that a rich man can be saved. We must devote our lives to God, not to our possessions. 'You cannot serve God *and* Wealth.'

His main teaching, then, is stewardship. He continually stresses that one day we must give an account of what we have done with our possessions. This is the teaching of the parables of the pounds and the talents. On this score he condemns the rich man who ignored the beggar, Lazarus, at his gate and the rich fool who, having made his pile, contemplated a purely self-indulgent retirement. How different a life is expected of those who serve God is made clear in his vivid portrayal of the Final Judgment in Matt. **25**, 31-46. And in brief, elsewhere (Luke **16**, 11 12) he says, 'If you have not proved trustworthy with the wealth of this world, who will trust you with the wealth that is real?'

Christ offers other occasional indications of this trustworthiness. We are not to broadcast our good works like the hypocrite (Matt. **6**, 2). We are to dispense our goods and services secretly 'not letting our left hand know what our right hand is doing'. In the incident of the widow's offering (Mark **12**, 41-44) he points out that our giving is measured by the sacrifice it entails - a hard principle!

We are not to worry about material things. In Matthew **6**, 19-34 he argues that since God really loves us he will take care of the future for us. If we worship money we shall have worries enough; if we worship God and trust in him, however strained our circumstances, we shall cope adequately with our day to day problems.

Christ's teaching about the Law and the Sabbath

In the chapter on Palestine (pp. 1-6) and in examining the Sermon on the Mount (pp. 38-43) we noted the great importance of the Law of Moses. It dominated the life of the Jews. The greatest sin for a Jew was to break the Law and those who openly did so were looked upon as outcasts by the Jewish leaders.

Here then is a summary of the situation in Christ's day with special reference to the Sabbath which was a continual source of trouble between Christ and the Pharisees.

The first five books of the Old Testament (the Torah) contained the Law which was absolute and could not be altered. In addition to the Law was its interpretation by the rabbis - its application to daily life. This body of interpretation was known as the Oral Law or the Tradition of the Elders, and had been compiled over many years. For example, the commandment to keep the Sabbath day holy had to be explained so that everyone should know what they could not do on the Sabbath, e.g. carry nails in their shoes ('a burden') and what they could do on the Sabbath, e.g. put a rough temporary bandage on a wound.

There were many hundreds of these regulations and keeping them was even more difficult because leading rabbis, Hillel and Shammai, disagreed about them. On some important subjects, such as divorce, there could be wide differences of opinion (see

p. 57). So complicated and numerous did the interpretations become that the common people found them almost impossible, and the Sadducees ignored them altogether.

The strictest Pharisees, on the other hand, seemed to spend most of their waking hours making sure that they broke none of them. In the Epistle of James (2, 10) we find it stated that 'whoever shall keep the whole law and yet stumble in one point has become guilty of all'. Pharisees who accepted this must have had little time for anything else but watching carefully what they did all day long. It was, they believed, their supreme duty to God.

Christ's interpretation of duty to God was wholly different. He recognised a weakness in his day that is common to all religions. Every religion involves both ceremonial and moral law. Now it is usually much easier to keep ceremonies than to practise morals. (Today, for example, it is easier to go to church regularly than to show real love towards a difficult neighbour.) This is precisely what had happened in Christ's day. The moral law had been obscured by multitudes of cermonies.

This applied especially to the Sabbath which in Jewish eyes was created by God himself (Gen. 2, 3). In fact some rabbis actually argued that God had created man in order to have someone to keep the Sabbath. The rules about the Sabbath were innumerable and it was the business of the rabbis in each community to see that everyone kept them as far as possible. Strict Jews still observe them. (The author himself can remember as a small boy being asked by a Jewess one Friday evening to go into her house, blow out four candles standing on the living room table and place them on the mantelpiece.)

It was the keeping of these ceremonial laws connected with 'work' on the Sabbath and, of course, attendance at the synagogue that sometimes caused real human need and suffering to be neglected on that day. On other days also custom and tradition could actually prevent the relief of suffering. (cf., the possible motives behind the indifference of the priest and Levite in the story of the good Samaritan).

Jesus repeatedly quarrelled with the authorities over this. 'If my disciples are hungry, why should they not reap a few grains of corn even if it is the Sabbath? If a man or woman is suffering why should he or she not be healed on the Sabbath day? The Sabbath was made for man, not man for the Sabbath! If it is necessary for me to lay hands on a leper to heal him or touch a corpse to restore it to life, what right has your ceremonial Law to prevent this relief of tragic suffering or sorrow?'

He was equally angry when he saw how traditional law was sometimes twisted even to do harm; when oaths were used to deceive (Matt. **23**, 16-22) or when money which should have gone to the support of aged parents was deliberately diverted to the Temple (Mark **7**, 9-13).

Christ judged the Oral Law solely by its usefulness. It had never to stand in the way of serving God or one's neighbour. And at times Jesus found it too trivial to bother about, as when his disciples failed to wash ceremonially before a meal (Mark **7**, 2).

The basic Law of Moses was, however, on a different plane. Jesus declared that he had come not to destroy but to fulfil it We find him keenly concerned about this in the Sermon on the Mount. (See pp. 38-43). Here are several examples of how he deepened and enriched its meaning, and how in some instances he modified it to conform to the needs of his day (Mark **10**, 2-10).

He himself concentrated on the moral law and offered the simplest directive ever given by a religious teacher to mankind: thou shalt love God and thy neighbour - Jew or Gentile.

The Pharisees' hostility to Christ

The Pharisees' objections to Christ are obvious:

1. They were jealous of his popularity, his mental ability - he always bettered them in argument - and his miraculous powers, which in exasperation they ascribed to the Devil. He was not one of them, having had no training in their colleges. In contrast to their white robes, their tassels, etc. he looked and dressed like a working man.

2. His claims really shocked them. He put himself in the place of God by claiming to forgive sins, to modify (fulfil) the Law of Moses, to be 'Lord of the Sabbath' and asserted that he was the Messiah (Nazareth and at his trial). Note some of his sayings: 'I am the Resurrection and the Life', 'He that hath seen me hath seen the Father', 'No man cometh to the Father save by me.'

3. He did not show them the respect they were used to. He condemned their hypocrisy and selfishness before the common people whom they were inclined to despise.

4. Especially did he ignore or condemn outright much of the oral tradition which they revered, such as the laws about the Sabbath, Corban, fasting and ceremonial washing. Any tradi-

tion that was useless or stood in the way of just dealing or compassion he swept to one side. The Pharisees, on the other hand, felt that by keeping the Oral Law in its entirety they would be recognised by Messiah, when he came, as God's special people.

5. He made friends with the common people. Instead of seeking the company of the Pharisees and lawyers, he lived and worked among the common people, choosing his disciples from them, making friends with tax-collectors, prostitutes and Gentiles. Because he enjoyed the company of such men as Zaccheus and Levi they denounced him as 'a glutton and a drunkard'.

Christ's objections to the Scribes and Pharisees.

Christ simplified religion - love God and your neighbour, he said. His disciples were therefore to express God's love in their relationships with everyone, whatever their class, race or creed. In the light of this teaching we can understand Christ's objection to the Scribes and Pharisees.

1. In place of love for their neighbour, they felt it more important to learn and keep the Oral Law. For instance, to tithe everything they possessed and bought, even down to a few seeds or stalks was a daily preoccupation (Matt. **23**, 23).

2. They were not above manipulating the Oral Law to cover injustice, as in the case of Corban (Mark **7**, 11) and the use of oaths (Matt. **5**, 33-37, Matt. **23**, 16-22). The lawyers among them took advantage of the weak to enrich themselves. (Luke **20**, 47).

3. They were self-centred and proud. They loved prominence: they prayed openly at street corners, disfigured their faces when fasting, wanted the chief seats in the synagogue and at feasts, and liked to hear themselves addressed as 'Rabbi' (Matt. **23**, 2-7, Matt. **6**, 2-16).

4. Some, no doubt, were kindly disposed towards their fellow-men, but the majority seemed to care very little for the common people and despised and shunned the really bad characters, such as tax-collectors and prostitutes and, of course, Gentiles. Jesus condemned them in such stories as that of the good Samaritan (Luke **10**, 25-37) and incidents such as Simon, the Pharisee (Luke **7**, 36-50).

5. Their attitude to John the Baptist angered Christ. He declared that they and their forebears had always behaved towards the

nation's prophets in that way (cf., The wicked husbandmen, Mark **12**, 1-12).

6. Very little in Christ's teaching about God, judgment and the after-life would they disagree with; Christ's condemnation centred on their failure to act upon it - like the man who built his house on sand (Matt. **7**, 26, 27).

The Gospel Miracles

More than thirty miracles are attributed to Jesus. Many people today, who otherwise are attracted to Christ's teaching, find them a stumbling-block. They demand scientific proof, and as there can be no such proof of Christ's miracles they are inclined to reject the whole story of the gospel.

The miracles do not present a real problem to the Christian because he accepts the greatest miracle of all, the Incarnation, that God, for a time, became man in the body of the carpenter of Nazareth.

The non-Christian is inclined to think that the miracles have been added to the story of Jesus to make him into a supernatural being with magical powers. But these miracles are then a strange effort at invention, because they are not at all like the stories usually told about fabulous people, such as the gods of Greece and Rome, or even the later magical stories told about Buddha. Note the following points:

1. Practically every miracle was performed to help someone in trouble. Never is Jesus recorded as performing a miracle to show his power, to help himself or merely to impress people.
2. The miracles are recorded in a down-to-earth, matter-of-fact way, not at all like the fanciful, exaggerated stories of legend.
3. Practically every miracle depended upon the faith of the person it helped. Jesus showed a knowledge of the power of mind over body that modern psychology is gradually bringing to light.
4. The miracles were taught to the Church within the lifetime of many people who lived with Jesus and were eye-witnesses of what he did -very sincere people who died often painfully for their beliefs and who would certainly have denounced anything false that was said about him.

The nature miracles (stilling the storm, feeding the five thousand) cause special difficulty because they so obviously contradict the laws of nature as we know them. But have we yet, in fact, discovered all the laws of nature?

The Resurrection is second only in importance to the Incarnation. Did it happen? Something, in fact, must have happened to transform eleven hopeless and frightened men into fearless witnesses to a living Christ. Some alternative theories are that:
1. The disciples stole the body and put about the story of the resurrection.
2. Jesus, in fact, was never dead.
3. The women and the disciples mistook the tomb and over the next six weeks suffered hallucinations.

None of these alternatives, however, will really stand up to close examination of the known facts about the early church.

On the other hand, an opinion worth noting is that of the late Baron Parker, who spent forty-seven years of his life in the Law as barrister and later as judge and was Lord Chief Justice of England from 1958 to 1971. Speaking to a group of business men he once declared, 'If in court I had to judge from the evidence whether Christ rose from the dead, I would conclude unquestionably that he did'.

Revision questions

1. Write an account of the incidents connected with *three* of the following:
   a. And the people were waiting for Zacharias and they wondered at his delay in the temple.
   b. There was no place for them in the inn.
   c. 'How is it that you sought me? Did you not know that I must be in my Father's house?'
   d. 'Man shall not live by bread alone'.
   e. 'Depart from me, for I am a sinful man, O Lord'.
2. Describe *two* occasions when John the Baptist or his disciples met Jesus.
3. Why were the Pharisees so hostile to the outcasts of society such as tax-collectors and prostitutes? Relate what happened in Simon the Pharisee's house, showing clearly the difference between Christ's and the Pharisee's attitude towards the woman visitor.
4. Describe the visit of Nicodemus to Christ. What do you think is especially important about this visit?
5. Relate the parable of the good Samaritan and describe the incident which led Jesus to tell the story.
6. Write down a saying of Jesus about a. humility; b. forgiveness. Then in each case relate a parable and an action of Jesus which illustrate his teaching on these subjects.
7. Describe *two* occasions on which Jesus healed people whom he did not actually meet and *one* which required great faith on the part of the person healed.
8. Describe all that happened in the garden of Gethsemane. Why would Jesus feel a very lonely person before and at his arrest?
9. Give a detailed account of Christ's trial before Pilate. Can anything be said in defence of Pilate? Give reasons for your answer.
10. Describe what happened to two of the disciples as they went to Emmaus and when they arrived there. Describe also another occasion when Jesus ate a meal with his disciples after his resurrection.

Ten-minute questions

1. Describe what happened at the inn in Bethlehem on the night Jesus was born.

2. Why did Joseph and Mary take Jesus to the temple forty days after his birth? What happened when they got there?
3. What, according to Matthew, did John the Baptist say to the Pharisees and Sadducees when they came to be baptised? What did they think of him?
4. What was the unforgiveable sin? How did the Pharisees commit this sin and how did Jesus reply to them?
5. Describe the feeding of the five thousand. What did Jesus and his disciples do after it was over?
6. Read Mark 3, 1-6.
   a. 'And they watched him' (v. 2). Who are 'they' in this sentence?
   b. Why would it be thought wrong for Jesus to heal this man?
   c. Why was Jesus angry?
   d. Who were the Herodians?
   e. Why is it strange that the Pharisees took council with the Herodians?
7. Three things Christ said in the Sermon on the Mount should be done secretly. What were they? What directions did Christ give to his followers in regard to them, and what particular habits of the Pharisees in these matters did he condemn?
8. Recount a parable Jesus told about prayer and say what you think it teaches us.
9. Imagine you were a spectator when Jesus cleared the Temple. Describe what you saw happening.
10. What very solemn action did Jesus take in the middle of his last meal with his disciples? How is it remembered today?
11. Who was the disciple who suddenly left the upper room during the Last Supper? Why did he go and what did he do after Jesus was arrested?
12. Describe the incident when Peter betrayed Jesus at his trial. Why did he behave in this way?
13. Write down two of Christ's utterances on the cross which showed his concern for other people and give reasons for them.
14. Describe briefly what happened on Easter morning at the tomb where Jesus was buried and the experiences of the first group of people who arrived there.
15. When the disciples announced that Christ had risen from death what action could Pilate or Caiaphas have taken to prove their story false if it had been so?

One-minute questions
1. What was the Annunciation?
2. What were the names of the two elderly people who greeted the baby Jesus in the Temple?

3. Can you spell the names of the three gifts the Wise Men brought to Jesus?
4. What did John the Baptist reply when Jesus asked to be baptised?
5. What did the boy Jesus reply when his parents found him in the temple and scolded him?
6. What town became the centre of Christ's ministry?
7. What did Jesus say to the paralysed man let down through the roof that made the Pharisees angry?
8. On what occasion did Jesus say to the Pharisees, 'Is it lawful on the Sabbath to do good or to do harm, to save life or to kill'?
9. What did the Geresene demoniac want to do when he was cured?
10. What were the two questions Jesus asked his disciples at Caesarea Philippi?
11. Name the two people who appeared with Jesus at his transfiguration and say what they represented.
12. Why did the rich young ruler feel sad when he left Jesus?
13. What was the request the mother of James and John made to Jesus?
14. Name two occasions during Christ's public life when a voice was heard speaking from heaven.
15. 'Wherever the gospel is preached in the whole world, what she has done will be told in memory of her.' Who was she and what had she done?
16. Name the High Priest and his father-in-law before whom Jesus was tried.
17. What did the chief priests do with the money that Judas returned to them?
18. To whom did Pilate send Jesus in the middle of his trial and why did he do so?
19. What was the name of the man who carried Christ's cross?
20. What did the centurion say when Jesus died?
21. How did Mary Magdalene recognise Jesus in the garden after his resurrection?
22. What was the last command Jesus gave his disciples on earth?
23. What did Jesus say great faith could do?
24. State *three* things Jesus told his disciples that the Holy Spirit would do for them.
25. Using one sentence for each briefly describe the following:

a. Sanhedrin	d. The High Priest	g. synagogue
b. The Law	e. Pharisees	h. Scribes
c. The Oral Law	f. Passover	i. Sadducees
		j. Procurator

Subject index

Index of Scripture Passages

JOHN

Some helpful books

Modern Texts
The Gospels in Modern English, J.B. Phillips, John Bertram, 1971.
The New English Bible, Oxford University Press or Cambridge University Press.
The Revised Standard Version, Collins.
The Common Bible.
The Gospel of Jesus, Greenlees, Theosophical Publishing House.
New World, Alan Dale, Oxford University Press.
The Jerusalem Bible, New Testament, Darton, Longman & Todd 1968.

Commentary
Understanding the Bible, vols. 4, 5, 6, R.E.P.
New Outlook Scripture: Book 1, Challenge of the Gospels, B.R. Youngman, Nelson.
The Story of the Scripture, vols 5, 7, Schofield & Sims.
The Synoptic Gospels, D.B.J. Campbell, John Murray, 1966.

The author has also published 500 questions on the life of Christ specially arranged for revision purposes, *Secondary Certificate Questions: The Life of Christ,* Methuen Educational, 1970.